The Infographic Resume

The Infographic Resume

How to Create a Visual Portfolio That Showcases Your Skills and Lands the Job

Hannah Morgan
Founder of Career Sherpa.net

McGraw Hill Education

New York Chicago San Francisco Athens London Madrid
Mexico City Milan New Delhi Singapore Sydney Toronto

1 2 3 4 5 6 7 8 9 0   DOC/DOC   1 2 0 9 8 7 6 5 4

ISBN   978-0-07-182557-3
MHID   0-07-182557-6

e-ISBN 978-0-07-182562-7
e-MHID   0-07-182562-2

McGraw-Hill Education books are available at special quantity discounts to use as premiums and sales promotions or for use in corporate training programs. To contact a representative, please visit the Contact Us pages at www.mhprofessional.com.

CONTENTS

CHAPTER 3	**Telling the Story of You**	**29**

CHAPTER 8   **Don't Overlook LinkedIn**   **143**

CHAPTER 11   Choose What You Share Online Carefully   183

ACKNOWLEDGMENTS

I am regularly surprised and awed by the amazing opportunities that seem to present themselves and the interconnectedness of people, places, and things in my world—all of which I am incredibly grateful for.

Collaborating with the team at McGraw-Hill Education is a prime example of what a small world we live in! Thank you to Tom Miller, Dannalie Diaz, and Casie Vogel, the talented editors at McGraw-Hill Education. Casie's excitement and encouraging words helped fuel the fire to collect and share this information on infographic and other new forms of resumes.

Thank you to the talented graphic designers and dedicated professionals who so willingly allowed me to feature their work in this book—and for the educational conversations that transpired along the way.

My brilliant connections in the recruiting and HR world continue to deliver great insight and filled in the background pieces to help make this book, what I hope will be seen as, a valuable resource. And I owe my humble gratitude to all the career professionals I follow and collaborate with to produce and share amazing work with job seekers.

I am increasingly inspired and curious about the future direction of recruitment and the use of images as well as alternative forms of communication between companies and those seeking employment. I hope, and think, we are on the cutting edge of a long series of advancements in improving the process across both sides of the desk.

Finally, thank you to my family who support me and my friends who endure me! Relationships are the web of life, and mine is incredibly strong because of all of you!

CHAPTER 1

How We Got Where We Are Today

Historically, job seekers have been required to respond to job postings by submitting a piece of paper (or two) to the organization with the opening. This piece of paper, known as a resume, is supposed to encapsulate the job seeker's work experiences, skills, and successes and then convince the reader to call and eventually hire the most qualified job seeker. This is the way it used to go, but today, due to a variety of circumstances, which this chapter will outline, the job seeker has to do more than submit a piece of paper in order to stand out and win the job.

The hiring process as we knew it is broken. Here are 10 ways today's job search has to be different and approached in a new way.

Changes in Hiring, Workforce, and Technology

1. The Death of the Paper Resume

You may have noticed fewer "help wanted" jobs that request you mail your resume and more employers at career fairs who do not accept hard-copy resumes. The old-fashioned hard-copy paper resume is fading away. It used to be you would type your resume on a typewriter, bring it to a copy shop, and have 100 copies made. Each time you applied for a job, you would type a cover letter, trifold it with the resume and stuff it in a number 10 envelope, seal it and put a stamp on it, travel to the mailbox, and wait.

That was a lot of work, it took time, and the cost of supplies and stamps meant that job seekers were somewhat more discriminatory about the jobs they applied for.

Too Many Applicants—Not Enough Time

Today, with several mouse clicks, some tweaking of electronic files, and data entry time, a job seeker could conceivably apply for hundreds of jobs in a single day.

So what does this mean for the companies doing the hiring? They are overwhelmed with applications and files with data to search and analyze. CareerXroads, a company that provides consulting and resources for corporate recruiters, has conducted a sources-of-hire study for the past 10 years. In the most recent report, information supplied by approximately 1,500 recruiters, human resources staff, and hiring managers across 250 companies was analyzed.[1] The summary report found the average job posting received 74 applications. Obviously, some jobs received more and some received less. Imagine reviewing 74 resumes and sifting that down to a manageable number of candidates to phone-screen.

With too many candidates to evaluate in a limited amount of time, recruiters and human resources staff are forced to focus on eliminating candidates rather than learning more about each one. It is estimated that about 50 percent of candidates are not qualified. This number sounds large, but maybe not, given this recent information. TheLadders conducted a study[2] asking people to review job postings. Using sophisticated eye-tracking technology, TheLadders found that 65 percent of the study participants who said they spent up to 10 minutes reading job postings were really only spending, on average, less than a minute per job posting. When the candidate did look at the description, the majority of the time spent was on the title, company name, and then job details (salary and recruiter information).

The resume isn't technically dead; you'll still need a text resume to apply using most systems online. But what the resume looks like is morphing, and the standard rules and guidelines are being challenged.

2. The Morphing of Job Boards and Resume Databases

Monster, CareerBuilder, and other mega job boards have replaced the help-wanted Sunday section of the newspaper. About 18 percent of new hires come from job boards like these, according the CareerXroads 2013 Sources of Hire study.[3] Companies searching for new employees pay to post and search the resume databases for candidates. These sources provide a talent pool to fish in; yet the talent swimming in this pool is not necessarily the best, nor are the data always up-to-date.

3

Job boards probably won't die either. Just like the rules for acceptable resumes have morphed, so too has how job boards operate. The decreasing cost of technology needed to manage job postings and collect applications has made it more affordable for companies to host their own job boards. Let's not forget the power of social networks and referral recruiting, which also have impacted the hiring process for the better. Companies can use their own site as a career portal, post opportunities on LinkedIn, or share through the social networks and talent pool communities.

3. The Dreaded Black Hole

Companies, small and large, have invested in an applicant tracking system, or ATS. This system allows them to manage job openings and screen incoming resumes from job seekers. The ATS serves as a massive database of applicant-supplied information. The job seekers enter the data when they apply and upload their resumes, which are parsed (diagnosed for keywords and broken into parts).

ATSs save time for busy HR professionals, but they seem like an impersonal middleman for job seekers. Often there is no e-mail address, name, or other contact information for the applicant to follow up with. As a result, job seekers have no way to ensure their documentation was received or even if the position is still available. Thus, they fall into the black hole of job applicants, void of communication.

This process is incredibly flawed. Good applicants who have poorly documented their skills get overlooked. Applicants try to game the system by adding tons of keywords in white font in the footer of their resumes, and worse, some applicants flat-out lie to catch the attention of the hiring company. While no system is perfect, when we put so much emphasis on a single document rather than the human being, everyone loses.

4. The Rise of Referrals

Hiring is a risky investment for a business. Job advertisements cost money, and it takes countless hours to screen and interview candidates. And there is no guarantee the new employee will work out. In fact, the cost to replace an employee is over 100 percent of his or her annual salary. That means if a $50,000 employee is fired or quits, it will cost another $50,000+ to hire a new employee, even if the first employee didn't last the full year.

One hiring method is less costly and risky. Referrals. Some companies offer employee referral bonuses. This means that if an employee refers a candidate or even if the candidate mentions the name of the employee who referred him or her for the job, that employee is compensated if or when the acquaintance is hired.

The *New York Times* reported in January 2013[4] that Ernst & Young had put more effort into its employee referrals and was striving to acquire close to 50 percent of its new hires from employee referrals. This same *New York Times* article reported that the quality of referred candidates was also better and so was the retention rate. In short, the article said that referred candidates make better hires!

5. Employer-Candidate Mismatch

Today's corporations, nonprofit organizations, and educational institutions (small and large) are crying for skills they say they cannot find. A study by DeVry's Career Advisory Group[5] asked 540 hiring managers if they could find candidates with the skills and personalities they were looking for. The results? The 2012 survey showed only 17 percent of hiring managers said nearly all or most job seekers have the skills and traits their company is looking for in a candidate.

It shouldn't be so hard to find the right candidate for the job with the tools and talent available. But when the resume is the primary and initial form of communicating such a complex message, it is no wonder the results are dismal.

6. Communication Mismatch

According to a Career Advisory Board study from 2011,[6] the skills and attributes employers value differ from the job seeker's self-assessment. The top skills valued by all employers across all job levels are accountability, time management, ability to work well with others, self-motivation, and strong work ethic. Yet the entry-level workers self-assess three out of these five skills higher than the employer

5

assesses the candidates it has seen. Is this because the entry-level candidates fail to demonstrate or communicate these skills or traits? And it isn't just entry-level candidates who assess their skills differently than employers see them—mid-level candidates self-assessed three out of the five skills higher than employers perceived them as well. These data might help explain the gap between what job seekers think and what the employer sees.

One vital component for job search success is to be well versed in the skills in demand for occupations as well as clearly understand the traits and personality types that match with specific company cultures.

7. The Gig Economy

There is no such thing as a permanent job any longer. Hiring temporary or contract workers is on the rise. In a survey by CareerBuilder,[7] 40 percent of employers said they planned to hire temporary and contract workers in 2013, up from 36 percent in 2012. As a matter of fact, employment agencies have renamed or reclassified the category of job where you start as a temporary employee for a period of time before you join the company payroll. The agencies used to call this "temp to perm," but permanent implies "forever" employment, which is no longer likely. Now, they call this transition work "temp to hire," which more accurately describes what happens.

Freelancers, consultants, and other independent workers account for approximately 35 to 40 percent of the private workforce in the United States. Roughly 43 million people are currently doing some type of contingent work, and this number is expected to grow to 65 million to 70 million within the decade.[8]

Companies create job openings based on new contracts or special projects that have a definitive end date. Hiring a contractor or temporary employee for a set amount of time saves the company money by not needing to pay health insurance benefits, vacation and other time off, and many other expenses that are incurred when a new employee walks into the office (phone, office supplies, technology, etc.).

6

The Gig Is Good

It is unstable, but the gig can also be highly fulfilling when you are in control of creating your own work. Gigs can also be good for your career. Each time you work a new gig in a new company with a new client and team, you are exposed to new processes, procedures, technology, people, and cultures. Exposure to all these things enriches your experience. Instead of just knowing how to do one thing one way, you now have a multitude of methods and styles to choose from. This breadth of exposure is marketable. It shows future employers your versatility. If a company has a specific project in mind for you, your additional experiences, skills, and knowledge add value, and this can be enticing to many employers, if you position it as such.

8. The Web as a Tool for the Masses

In the early days of websites, only large corporations with the money and resources could afford a website. A business's website served as an online sales brochure. The content seldom changed. This was back in the day of dial-up Internet when it would often take minutes to connect to the Internet and for the website to display.

The Internet continued to evolve and slowly became a tool for anyone to use. WordPress blogs, YouTube videos, and thousands of other free applications provide anyone with Internet access the ability to create websites and videos, share pictures, and interact online. Owning and creating a website, which was once out of reach financially and technologically for most people, is now possible for anyone to do.

And let's not forget that 56 percent of U.S. adults walk around with instant access to the web through smartphones.[9]

9. Trend Setters as Trailblazers

There have always been early adopters and people ahead of their time. These people have blazed fresh trails, enabling others to follow. It is the work of those early adopters, coupled with the competition for jobs, that puts us in a place where we have to do more to compete for the work available today.

Information Technology Got It Long Ago

You may not remember the first tech bubble boom and bust in the 1980s. Tech start-ups were in their infancy during this period, operating lean and mean and without a host of lifetime employees. What they had instead were hungry, eager, highly skilled talent, joined by their passion and commitment to produce an amazing product.

These choice jobs only went to the best and the brightest and commanded good money. What this proved was that when risk and reward were key to a project, it had the potential to produce amazing results.

Both parties understood that the work arrangement was temporary and would last until the release of the product. There was an unspoken agreement that if their work was great, they may be invited to stay on; otherwise, they eagerly moved on to a new project, thereby broadening their experience and portfolio of skills and increasing their demand. By the way, this also tended to increase their potential earning power. Word-of-mouth referrals and personal reputation meant a lot.

Actors and Artists Led the Way

A head shot in a black carrying case was the staple of every actor, actress, and model. And artists carried their oversized portfolios with samples of their work as real-time examples or proof. The photo along with the prestige of their previous work assignments and samples of work helped them secure future gigs. But it was and is the audition that seals the deal. Seeing is believing. Therefore, their performance made the biggest impact. Artists produce visual proof of their work and creativity. The audition, or tryout, is something the normal working person traditionally doesn't have the opportunity to perform. Instead, we have the event—or interview. But what if our performance were evaluated differently? What if we could be evaluated by actually seeing what we are doing in real time?

CEOs Got It Too

Those people on track to be a CEO spend as much time building their network and managing their reputation as they do running their company. They work at networking and building the right relationships because they know that a gig as a CEO is finite—either by their choice or by the choice of the board of directors. CEOs and CEOs-to-be are always looking for their next great gig, and they manage their personal reputation and performance as carefully as their company does. So should you.

Sheryl Sandberg's rise to COO of Facebook was no coincidence. Her impressive work history might have qualified her for the job, working for Google and for the U.S. Secretary of the Treasury as chief of staff. But what really got her where she is today? Yes, her Harvard MBA didn't hurt either. But it was Sandberg's connections that helped open the door for her at the Treasury Department through Larry Summers, whom she worked for out of college.[10]

As Sandberg said in her Barnard commencement speech, "It is the ultimate luxury to combine passion and contribution. It's also a very clear path to happiness."[11] What if there were a way to use all the resources and tricks used by CEOs, IT professionals, and actors and artists?

10. The Rise of LinkedIn

LinkedIn was launched in 2003[12] as a professional social network. It has become a place where working professionals can interact, exchange information, and, most importantly, stay connected despite changes in jobs and e-mail addresses. Users create a profile including at a minimum their work experience and education. Braver users may add their photograph and links to movies, presentations, and other samples of work. As more users have jumped on and LinkedIn has added features and functionality to its network, it has become widely embraced by over 300 million users across the globe.[13] For some, it is their one-stop source for professional news and updates. For others, it serves as a platform for launching their job search campaign. Companies have embraced LinkedIn as a resource for finding talent, not only active job seekers, but passive, content employees as well. Anyone with a profile on LinkedIn is searchable, making it easier for recruiters, human resources, and anyone else searching for a new employee to access this massive database in order to find the person with the unique blend of skills and experience desired.

Given these circumstances and the new state of our economy and workforce, there is just one solution—build an online portfolio.

9

Power to the People—
Look Like a Rock Star

You have the tools and power to build an online presence; no longer should you feel limited to the single-page, paper list of job titles, dates, and duties. There is so much more to tell and so many ways to prove your expertise. But with this power comes more responsibility to manage your career destiny. Proactively marketing your skills and taking ownership for this requires a new way of thinking.

New Thinking

If you are ready to embrace the idea that you are in charge of managing your career and professional reputation and accomplishments, then you will also need to develop more skills. In a way, you are now the owner of your own business, and that comes with a multitude of responsibilities. Consider this the quick study guide for learning about the most important areas of each job title.

The Many Hats You'll Wear
You will need to think like a:

- **Business owner.** If you consider your career as your business, that assumes responsibility for its profitable growth and operation.
- **Graphic artist.** Developing visual content (infographics, photos, logos, etc.) is increasingly important to your online reputation. Visuals and multimedia are becoming more popular and increase readability.
- **Public relations specialist.** Managing your online reputation should be as important to you as it is to a company. This includes anything from developing publicity campaigns (such as your job search) to dissolving any negative information about you.
- **Marketing manager.** Creating unique branding and recognition and strategies for growing your visibility will enhance your career.
- **Sales representative.** Learning and using consultative selling will help you to manage your career at all times.

- **Copywriter.** Writing convincing material; creating compelling copy; and preparing interesting bios, profiles, and persuasive e-mails all fall under your responsibility now.
- **Photographer.** You need to know enough about photography to take good photos and make sure good photos are taken of you.
- **Website designer.** Laying out readable, visually enticing web content will improve the popularity of your own site, and knowing the tools and resources available gives you the bells and whistles of the big-time designers.
- **Search engine mastermind.** Knowledge of search engine optimization ensures that anything you post or create online will maximize the right tags and keywords to make it easily found when someone is searching the Internet.
- **Business consultant.** Whatever occupation you pursue, consider yourself a consultant in that area. You need to stay up on trends and provide solutions; you are more than just an employee, and you must deliver results.
- **Hiring manager.** A hiring manager is the person whom you will ultimately report to, but you should also think like human resources staff and third-party recruiters, so you can deliver your message and qualifications in terms they will relate to and appreciate.

Your Strategy for Success

This book provides instruction and examples to help all job seekers, from a new graduate through a seasoned professional, learn to market themselves to stand out and better quantify their experiences and success. And it all starts with building a strategy—your plan for what, when, where, why, and how you will build your online (and offline) portfolio.

As the great Dr. Seuss said in *Oh, the Places You'll Go!*:

You're off to Great Places!
Today is your day!

CHAPTER 2

Your Online Portfolio

Traditionally, portfolios were for actors, models, artists, and other creative professions. But today, just about anyone, and everyone, can show his or her work.

If you are serious about treating your career like a business, then you'll need a place on the web to show your work and build an online identity, just like every other business does. Your online portfolio may be a personal website or your LinkedIn profile, or it may be a virtual portfolio containing examples of work showcased on creative portfolio communities.

This chapter will explore the different options you will want to consider and, more importantly, why you should consider creating an online portfolio.

How to get on someone's radar

Playing by the rules has always been an important business strategy, but so is standing out. So what do you need to know to stand out? The job application process and workarounds may be different for a small versus a large company. Glassdoor's Talent Warrior Award recognized Carrie Corbin, associate director of talent management at AT&T, for most innovative and socially active recruiter.[1] When Glassdoor asked her how someone could get on her radar, Corbin recommended trying to contact someone directly when applying for a position in a smaller company; however, with a larger company, Corbin said circumventing the process may send the wrong message. Corbin says "standing out would be creating a resume and/or work examples that clearly call out and QUANTIFY your experience and accomplishments that relate to the job you're applying for." And if you are in creative fields or marketing, Corbin recommends a portfolio with real examples to showcase your work.

What Will You Include in Your Portfolio?

Begin thinking about what you want to include in your portfolio, either an online collection of works or samples you keep for your own documentation. The options are truly endless. This is where you get to put on several hats: PR, marketing, graphic designer, and copywriter. If you see yourself as if you are a business, it will help you to think outside the "employee box." In other words, thinking like a business owner helps you see yourself in new ways—you had an impact on your employer by solving problems and instituting solutions. Most importantly, you are more than just a cog in a wheel; you are a complex human with multiple talents and contributions that make a difference.

Whether you're creating an online portfolio or just thinking about what you should be collecting, this list of items should help provide some direction:

PORTFOLIO CONTENTS

- Samples of your work
- Headshot
- Bio or summary
- Text and infographic resumes
- Social media outlet links
- Letters of recommendation or testimonials
- Satisfied customer and client e-mails
- Awards or recognition
- Special projects
- Volunteer involvement

Your challenge is to think like the marketing department at a big corporation like Coke, Ford, or the *New York Times*. Company websites and commercials contain customer testimonials, product demonstrations, and proof of their products. Companies are doing much more than stagnant print advertising, and with the power of the Internet, so can you! It just takes a little creativity—okay maybe more than just a little, but you can do it!

15

What to Showcase

Think about the problems you've solved at work, not your daily job duties. What differentiates you from the hundreds and thousands of other people who have the same job title as you?

- Is there a picture of you receiving an award?
- Have you given a presentation or spoken at a conference?
- Have you written articles?

What would you want people to find if they were searching for you on the web? These are the images, articles, and content you can create and publish yourself online. *Hint:* You may want to begin capturing screenshots, saving links mentioning you, and documenting the projects you contributed to.

Samples of Work

Graphic artists and website designers have visual proof of their work; it is their deliverable. However, if you are a customer service specialist, software tester, inside sales representative, accounts receivable processor, or administrative assistant, your output or deliverables are less obvious and may not initially be seen as visual. Here are some ideas you may not have thought about:

- Process flowchart
- Photograph of new in-store product display
- Summary of your call metrics
- Reports, procedures, or training created and delivered

Start by thinking about something you did that you were proud about. Document the entire story, and you are likely to uncover some illustration, document, or material you can use as a sample of your work.

One word of caution: Do not share confidential or proprietary information or materials. You might be able to re-create a generic version of the material, omitting specific details or proprietary information. Just be sure to note that the document is a re-creation. Believe it or not, your integrity is at risk. Many people and companies can be hypersensitive about protecting sensitive information. Your integrity is being evaluated.

Not Sure What Samples to Include?

Collecting the right work samples and examples is hard work. To make sure you are on track and amassing the right material, skim through job postings you are interested in and look for reoccurring skill sets and technical skill requirements. Better yet, arrange an informational meeting with someone inside a company you would like to work for and learn what skills, projects, experiences, knowledge, and personality type the company looks for in the person who performs the job you are interested in. Here are just a few examples:

"Create and/or deliver presentations . . ."
Re-create or adapt a presentation you have given or created.

"Develop and write summary of . . ."
Show your writing sample for any type of summary you have written, perhaps a book review, compilation of research data, or client case study.

"Conduct research on . . ."
Show your research outline or map the process used to conduct a research project.

"Resolve customer issues"
Include a testimonial from a happy customer or excerpt from a manager's performance review citing your customer service performance.

"Manage project details"
Show a project timeline, Gantt chart, or diagram showing the flow of people, resources, and activities.

"Calculate/analyze"

Use examples of spreadsheets or output from SPSS, SASS, or other statistical or analytical software.

"Troubleshoot"

Show a decision matrix or if-then flowchart outlining your thought process.

"Manage, mentor, lead"

Use sample training plans, performance methodology, or evaluation system used in directing others.

Have these given you some ideas? When reviewing these postings, also note the requested adjectives or personality traits. This will help you determine the tone and style for your delivery.

I've Got Nothing

If you don't have anything, don't throw the towel in yet. There are options—create something! Here are some ideas to help you create portfolio-building material:

- Create a mock-up or sample report, summary, or flowchart to prove you have the skills.
- Use personal samples (personal budget, scheduling calendar, personal website, etc.).
- Volunteer with a nonprofit, family, friend, or neighbor to deliver a project that you can use to document.

Headshot

A professional photograph is a must-have in today's socially connected world. It's placed on your web page, social network profiles, and maybe even your resume and business card. You will learn what makes a good headshot and find other tips about taking pictures in Chapter 3.

Your Bio or Summary

A short and longer version of who you are, what you've accomplished, and what your goals are is helpful in telling your overall story. These important elements of your portfolio are more than just a career overview—they are your pitch. You'll learn more in Chapter 3.

Resume

Many applicant tracking systems and hiring professionals still prefer to see a resume in a text format, so a traditional text version of your resume is still important. However, you now have more options for creating a resume in the form of infographic resumes, interactive resumes, presentation resumes, and graphic design resumes. You'll see samples of these new forms of resumes throughout this book.

Social Media Outlet Links

Perhaps you are already professionally active on social networks. Promoting links to your activity on these channels offers greater insight into your communication style, interests, and personality. A social media presence also demonstrates your expertise and thought leadership. When you are active on social media, your status updates offer another way to share news with your network. Learn about sharing your information through social media in Chapter 9.

Letters of Recommendation

Asking for and receiving letters of recommendation is not as popular as it once was. This is the case partially because no one would ever write a poor recommendation for someone, and also LinkedIn's recommendation feature makes it easier to give and receive recommendations. What good would these letters be if they were in a file on your desk. Acquiring a testimonial is a valuable way of proving what people thought about your work.

Satisfied Customer and Client E-mails

The hope is that you have been keeping these e-mails in your personal folder at home (not on your work computer). If not, you can try

19

to contact past customers or clients and remind them of the work you did with them and ask if they would be willing to write a letter of recommendation or a message about the specific solution you provided them. These are another form of testimonial.

Awards or Recognition

Public recognition is rewarding personally and professionally. If you have received performance awards, recognition for your ideas, or other formal awards, make a copy or take an electronic screenshot.

Special Projects

Were there instances where you went beyond your scope of work on special projects in school, in your department, or at your company? Showcase these projects with pictures, samples of work, or written feedback. These projects can demonstrate your willingness to go above and beyond as well as support your expertise in certain areas.

Volunteer Involvement

Investing your personal time in activities can also show your dedication or emphasize other areas of interest. Don't discount your unpaid work.

* * *

Now that you know the elements of your portfolio, let's take a look at how to best organize your website, which will eventually host all these elements.

The Best Portfolio Is One You Own: Claim Your Domain

Where is the one place online you want people to go to learn more about you? Think carefully about this. If you take a shortcut and answer "LinkedIn" because it is easy, fast, and free, think again. You don't own your profile on LinkedIn; LinkedIn does. Think about creating your own website instead. You don't have to be a technical geek;

however, there is a small learning curve. (But this is building skills!) Consider the relatively small cost of owning a website to ensure you control your online identity. This seems the clear and popular choice of motivated careerists and professionals.

Buy the URL

Uniform resource locator, or URL, is the technical term for a web address. Search a domain registrar such as Namecheap.com, Hover .com, Name.com, or GoDaddy.com to see if your name is available. Also try to get the ".com" extension, though that doesn't matter as much as it used to. If your name is not available, try adding your middle initial or designatory letters; these are the letters after your name that represent educational degree, accreditation, office, or honor. For example, if you completed your MBA, you might choose "Jane Doe MBA" as your web address. If that is not available or you do not have any special designation, try using your middle initial or middle name such as "Jane Smith Doe." The cost to own your domain name is roughly $15 a year.

Option 1: Create Your Site

You could build your site from a template website or use a WordPress self-hosted site (http://www.wordpress.org). WordPress is the preferred platform by many socially savvy professionals and therefore should be good enough for you as well. Tumblr (http://www.tumblr .com) is another microblogging site that professionals use to share their written thoughts, photos, and samples of work. If you have greater technical savvy, you may be brave enough to create your own website from scratch. Ask your colleagues or other professionals you know to see what website provider they recommend.

You will need a service to host your URL and website on its servers. Here are some popular website hosting providers: Dreamhost, Hostgator, Bluehost, and Linode. The annual cost for a hosting service is about $50.

What comes next? Selecting the right pages and content for your virtual portfolio!

21

Pages for Your Online Portfolio or Website

If you browse through websites, you will notice many share the same or similar page titles. That's because they work and readers come to expect certain categories. Here are the most popular web-page categories. You can include additional pages or delete the ones that don't apply (yet).

Home Page

Every site needs an easy-to-navigate home page. The content on this page will help visitors get a quick overview of you and what action you would like them to take (where they can go to learn more about you).

About Page

Your about page tells your story. It is often written in the first person and should demonstrate your personality and style and include important information you need your readers to know about you. It may chronicle your work experience, and you can include links to both a text and infographic version of your resume. This is particularly helpful for those who may want to see (and download) the traditional document. If you are a photographer, musician, or artist, you may have an artist's statement, which explains your style of work. You may even choose to include a link on your about page to your visual or social resume.

Portfolio Page

Your portfolio can show samples of your completed projects (paid or unpaid). It can be as focused or broad as you want it to be, depending on the type of work you want to do. For example, a photographer who takes senior portraits and wedding pictures would include the best examples from those categories. A project manager who only wants to do IT-type or software development–type work would include project plans and program write-ups only on the types of projects he or she wants to work on. A project manager who no longer wants to do event planning work can leave off that type of work. Think about showing pictures, company logos, and samples of work.

SERVICES AND SPECIALTIES

Consider this section or page a list of your key skills and expertise. Here is where you outline specifically what types of work you excel at and want to do.

PROJECTS

If you worked on special volunteer or school projects, this would be a spot to include them. Again, think about showing the visual proof of your work. Use photos from the event or product launch or maybe a photo of the team working together during a tight deadline. Be as specific as possible and remember to include the outcome or results of the work you did. Quantify with numbers whenever possible.

News Page or Blog

You can use your blog to draw attention to significant events, news, or projects. If you've been published or speak publicly, there are probably press releases and announcements you would want to list, either chronologically or by topic. Additionally, if you've been written about in a newsletter, local publication, or elsewhere, include a link to that page or take a screenshot and save it as an image online.

Contact Page

Last, but certainly not least, include multiple ways for people to contact you. If you do not want to list your e-mail address or phone number, you should use a contact form that people can use to reach out to you. Make it easy for your reader to contact you. While you may prefer to be contacted by e-mail or your social network of choice, your future client may be more comfortable making a phone call. Including multiple contact mechanisms helps make it easy for all sorts of people to contact you. If you do list your e-mail address, it should sound professional. If you have a personal URL, you can usually get one e-mail address for free. This would be the best option. Another option would be to use a web-based e-mail provider, such as Gmail, that will allow you to access it on the go.

Option 2: Use Creative Portfolio Platforms and Communities

The following portfolio communities are designed to support the creative work from illustrators, photographers, copywriters, art directors, character designers, fashion designers, graphic designers, web designers, logo designers, typographers, interior designers, concept artists, architects, product designers, and stylists as well as almost anyone else who would like to show their work projects. Recruiters and business owners can easily search these sites to source the talent and skill sets they need.

Behance (http://www.behance.net)

The Behance network is free to sign up and provides a direct link to your portfolio for sharing across other platforms. Your work on Behance can also be included in your LinkedIn profile. Your portfolio contains a bio, headshot, links to social networks, focus or areas of expertise, number of likes and views on your projects and uploaded work, and a section to include your work history.

Carbonmade (http://www.carbonmade.com)

Carbonmade showcases work by a wide variety of creatives. Your individual portfolio is customizable and contains a bio, headshot, links to social networks, list of your specialties, and direct link to your work. You can also specify your work status. Sign-up is free with the option to upgrade, which enables you to connect your portfolio to a custom domain such as http://www.yourname.com.

DeviantArt (http://www.deviantart.com)

DeviantArt is an online community showcasing various forms of user-made artwork. Popular forms of work include digital art, traditional art, photography, illustrations, anime, wallpapers, skins, and more. A direct portfolio link is provided to help share your work on other sites. Your deviant profile includes a headshot, interests (or specialties), location, and number of views. This site is a community where people ask for feedback and comment on work. The basic sign-up is free.

Dribbble (http://dribbble.com)

Dribbble is a community of web designers, graphic designers, illustrators, icon artists, typographers, logo designers, and other visual creative types sharing small screenshots that show their work, process, and current projects. Each shot or upload can be tagged to highlight skills and tools used to create the work. Each shot or upload includes the number of views, likes, and comments. The artist profile includes a headshot, location, links to website and social networks, and a mini bio section.

GitHub (http://github.com)

If you develop code or you program, you'll want to add your work to this community. GitHub offers both paid plans for private repositories and free accounts for open-source projects. The site provides social networking functionality such as feeds, followers, and a social network graph to display how developers work on their versions of a repository.

Sample Portfolios

Kevin Luu is a DJ, music producer, recording/mixing engineer, sound designer, musician, and studio maintenance technician. Even before he graduated from Berklee College of Music, he established his virtual portfolio. As his career grew, so has his collection of work assignments, which he captures in photos on his home page and lists on the pages within his virtual portfolio. (See Figure 2-1.)

FIGURE 2-1
Kevin Luu
Portfolio
http://www.kluumusic
.com;
http://bit.ly/1ak7ZxR

Robin Flanigan is a freelance writer who has chosen to visually highlight her published work, giving it extra appeal. Her portfolio includes her work as it appears in magazines, in newspapers, in brochures, on the web, and in several of her published books. Featured images from the publications and pdf files showcase her writing style. Her portfolio also provides testimonials that give even more credibility to her professionalism and offer insight into her work. (See Figure 2-2.)

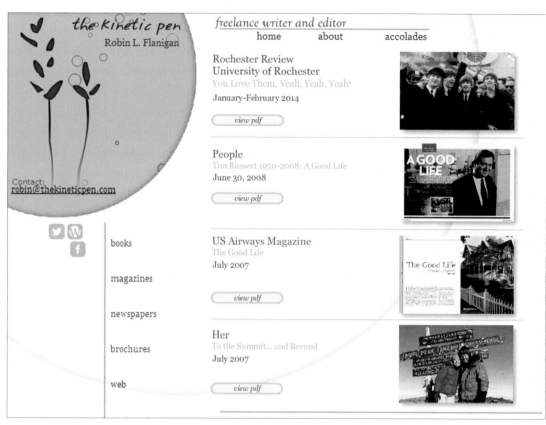

FIGURE 2-2
**Robin Flanigan's
Portfolio**
http://www
.thekineticpen.com;
http://bit.ly/1k0q5bP

27

CHAPTER 3

Telling the Story of You

Your series of life experiences is your story. Everything you have done has made you who you are today. The challenge that you, just like most other people, face is conveying your story in a way that is meaningful to those reading it or hearing it—your audience. Traditionally, you told your work story on a single sheet of resume paper. Luckily there are new alternatives today. But creating your story in any format requires that you organize and prioritize and build the most compelling and relevant story so it grabs your readers' attention and makes them want to take action.

There are lots of options, opinions, and styles for creating your story. In this chapter we'll look at what you can do to create an interesting story, one that is a true reflection of who you are, crystallizes what you want to be known for, and differentiates you from the competition. First you'll have to do the heavy lifting and think about the parts of your story you want to tell.

Inventory Your Assets

It all starts by creating lists of your personality traits, technical skills, industry experience, projects, and accomplishments.

Hagan Blount, designer, suggests asking yourself these sets of questions as you think about inventorying your assets:

> What are the aspects of your career that can be boiled down to more meaningful metrics? Anyone that's been hired to work has always been hired to improve on ROI. How did you improve on your last company's ROI? What do you do, what task did you perform, what repetitive motion did you execute that brought the company ROI from the salary that they paid you? This is really the most important question you can ask yourself in coming up with ideas for an actual infographic. Some people may rely on creative ways to show a skill set or a career path when the bottom line is always: what can you add to the bottom line?

Personality Traits

By no means is the following list an all-inclusive one. It should, however, help you choose a unique combination of words to describe your personality. Identify three to five you feel best describe you. Though these descriptors alone do not make you unique or a standout candidate, the combination starts the process of describing who you are. Be sure you select your strongest personality traits—the ones that appear in your past performance reviews, that are used in letters of recommendation, or that you regularly hear your coworkers use to describe you.

Accountable	Adaptable	Adventurous
Alert	Ambitious	Appropriate
Assertive	Astute	Attentive
Authentic	Aware	Brave
Calm	Candid	Capable
Certain	Charismatic	Clear
Collaborative	Committed	Connected
Compassionate	Conscious	Considerate
Consistent	Cooperative	Courageous
Creative	Curious	Dedicated
Determined	Diplomatic	Disciplined
Dynamic	Easygoing	Effective
Efficient	Empowering	Empathetic
Energetic	Ethical	Enthusiastic
Excited	Expressive	Faithful
Fearless	Fair	Friendly
Flexible	Generous	Happy
Honest	Honorable	Humorous
Imaginative	Immaculate	Independent
Industrious	Innovative	Interesting
Intelligent	Intentional	Joyful
Knowledgeable	Lively	Logical
Loving	Loyal	Nurturing
Open-minded	Optimistic	Organized

Patient	Peaceful	Playful
Poised	Polite	Powerful
Practical	Proactive	Problem solving
Productive	Punctual	Reliable
Resourceful	Responsible	Self-confident
Self-reliant	Sincere	Skillful
Spiritual	Spontaneous	Stable
Strong	Successful	Supportive
Tactful	Trusting	Trustworthy
Truthful	Versatile	Vibrant
Warm	Willing	Wise
Zealous		

In Chapter 7, you'll see how these personality traits can be incorporated into infographic resumes and help differentiate you or at least provide greater insight into who you are. You may choose to list traits in your summary section, reference them as a list within a "qualities" or related category on your resume, show the level of your personality trait as a bar graph, or even include testimonials from others who have used one or more traits to describe you.

Your Technical Skills

These are work-related things you know how to do. Technical skills in accounting might include month-end and year-end reports, bank reconciliation, general ledger, fixed assets, and trial balance. Don't just say accounting, because that isn't specific enough.

Each occupation has its own list of must-know and in-demand skills. You can also check job descriptions to make sure your inventory is complete. And by the way, if you are missing any in-demand skills, make note and plan on developing or acquiring those skills ASAP.

You will see the myriad of ways to highlight technical skills in Chapter 7. Icons, buttons, or logos can represent specific computer languages. The level of expertise could be demonstrated as a bar graph, or you could even represent you growth over time or cumulative skill as an area graph.

Industry Experience

What industries have you worked in? Often, it is your breadth and depth of industry knowledge that will help differentiate you. Create a list of all the industries you can claim knowledge in. If you are new to the workforce, begin researching different industries and identify ones that seem interesting and offer possible opportunities for you.

Once you've compiled your list of industries, think about pictures or images that would clearly and universally represent each one. For example, someone in the food and beverage industry may find an image of a plate and glass. Or someone in the telecommunications industry might use a picture of a phone or cell phone.

Projects

Create a list of the projects you've worked on. What was their purpose, and what was your role? Also note what the project's outcome or results were. These projects can be work related, projects related to school, or even volunteer projects.

Accomplishments

Every day you made a difference. These differences are called accomplishments, and they can be big or small. This next list should help you begin brainstorming the important achievements you want to highlight.

Your past performance is indicative of future performance. Use the questions below as prompts to help you remember your accomplishments. This isn't easy, so if you are having difficulty, consult with a coworker or someone who knows your work.

- What were you proud of doing at work?
- What did you do better than others around you?
- Were you ever recognized (formally or informally) for work that you did?
- Did you ever go above and beyond what was required of you?
- Were you ever selected to be a part of a team or train others?
- Did you identify and solve a problem?
- Did you save time and/or money?

33

- Have you improved productivity?
- Have you ever streamlined operations?
- Did you devise new strategies?
- Did you minimize customer complaints?
- Did you provide a service that did not exist before?
- Did you develop an idea that was used or presented?
- Did you help others achieve their goals?

A Framework for Documenting Your Accomplishment

In one sentence or less, describe the situation or setup for your accomplishment. Next, describe the task you were faced with. Then describe the actions *you* specifically took (step-by-step). Finally, state the outcome or result of your work and the situation. Use quantifiable data; even estimate if necessary to show the measurable impact your work had.

Situation: _____

Task: _____

Actions: _____

Result: _____

_____

_____

Summing It Up

All the work you just completed will help you create your story, infographic, or visual resume and, most importantly, showcase the best of what you have to offer.

> The story is your ability to effect change within an organization. It's the ability to take the process that's successful at 20 percent and make it successful at 40 percent. It's the ability to reduce the amount of time that the process takes by 20 percent. It's the ability to improve the amount of callbacks that are received by 20 percent. It's the ability to increase the number of sales that are made by 20 percent. It's the ability to increase the per call average by 20 percent. It's the ability to get your reps to take 20 percent more opportunities. It's the ability to clean 20 percent more floors or empty 20 percent more wastebaskets per night. Whatever task you're performing at the organization, it can be quantified, and you can be the superstar of that function. Find out what you add to the bottom line.
>
> **—HAGAN BLOUNT,** infographic resume writer and designer

A System for Explaining

Lee LeFever is the founder of Common Craft and author of *The Art of Explanation*. Common Craft began making videos in 2007 to explain things like technology. Early videos explained how Twitter and DropBox worked so that people could understand new or more difficult concepts. Based on Lee's experience creating videos, he writes and speaks about how to improve how we communicate ideas with the goal to help people understand. These are some of the key points Lee makes in his presentations about the concept of explaining things:

35

- **Have empathy—put yourself in the shoes of your audience.** Your audience is human resources, recruiters, screeners, hiring managers, or anyone else who has been tasked with reviewing hundreds of resumes on top of an already overfilled plate of duties and emergencies. Recognizing your audience and their responsibilities will help you understand the people you are writing for and why you need to show empathy toward them and the companies they represent, which are also facing regular crises, decreasing budgets, and too much work to handle.
- **Realize that knowledge is a curse!** "The more we know, the harder it is to imagine what it is like *not* to know," says Lee. Review every word you use and don't assume your audience understands what a word means. This can be especially difficult when the subject matter is you. Step back, reevaluate your word selection, and get feedback from others.
- **Build context and make your audience care.** Context means you give an easy definition that everyone can understand. Provide a real-world problem that the people in your audience will relate to, and by creating this connection, they will begin to care about what you are going to say next. It draws them in or acts as the hook.
- **Tell a story.** The simple short story gives the audience a situation it can relate to. Here is an example Lee used: "Meet Bob. Bob has a problem. Bob finds the solution. Bob is happy. Go Bob!" (Your audience is thinking, "I've got that problem too!")
- **Use an analogy.** Lee uses this as an example of how an analogy can help your audience understand a new concept: "It's just like *Jaws* in space" (George Lucas explaining *Star Wars*), or you could model your analogy after Steve Jobs's introduction of the iPod. He said, "iPod. One thousand songs in your pocket."
- **Make the connection—link your story in an agreement statement.** "I think we can all agree that time is precious. You want to make money. You are a business owner, not a social media guru."
- **Be remarkable.** Use media (video, audio, images). At this time, not all the candidates are using media to supplement their stories.

By doing so, you are in the minority and, thus, remarkable, or at least memorable.

As you can see, there is a lot to consider when explaining, especially if what you are explaining is your career and you. Keeping your audience in mind is important. The way to tell your story will vary based on who your audience is. It isn't a one-size-fits-all solution. This is why having just one version of your resume doesn't work in today's job search. Your story doesn't change, but the words you choose to use will. Even Lee agrees that it is important to be remarkable and recommends using video, audio, and/or images to translate your message. The act of simplifying how you explain who you are and what you do by boiling it down to the most important, shareable tidbits of information helps you focus and prioritize key points.

The Pitch

Another, shorter, way to present yourself is by using a pitch. Yes, it reeks of sales, and that is where it originates from—the sales pitch. Daniel H. Pink, author of *To Sell Is Human: The Surprising Truth About Moving Others,* explains:

> The purpose of the pitch isn't necessarily to move others immediately to adopt your idea. The purpose is to offer something so compelling that it begins a conversation, brings the other person in as a participant and eventually arrives at an outcome that appeals to both of you.[1]

One of the pitches Daniel describes in his book is the Pixar pitch. Pixar Animation Studios has won six academy awards for its films *Finding Nemo, The Incredibles, Ratatouille, WALL-E, Up,* and *Toy Story 3.* According to Daniel, Emma Coats, a former story artist at Pixar, analyzed what made Pixar films so successful. Apparently, they share the same narrative DNA, as Daniel calls it. These six sentences apply to any of the Pixar movie storylines and would make a nice script for your infographic or presentation resume.

Once upon a time _____.
Every day, _____.

One day _____. Because of that,
_____.

Because of that, _____. Until finally,
_____.[2]

Just in case you aren't familiar with any of the Pixar movie plots, Daniel shared the storyline for *Finding Nemo* in his book. It starts with: "Once upon a time there was a widowed fish named Marlin who was extremely protective of his only son, Nemo. Every day, Marlin warned Nemo of the ocean's dangers and implored him not to swim far away."[3]

As the rest of the story goes, Nemo ventures out into the ocean and is captured by a diver, and Marlin begins a quest to find his son. The story has a happy ending, and Nemo and his father are reunited after a series of adventures and encounters with other sea creatures.

What do you offer that is so compelling that it begins a conversation? This is a difficult question and can be hard to show on a standard, text-based resume. Think about a project you worked on for a recognized customer. Showing the customer's logo on your visual resume may be very attractive to a competitive company or someone who recognizes or admires the work of that brand. You are now affiliated with that brand, if you choose to show it on your visual resume. Your pitch is the answer to "What do you do?" or "Tell me about yourself." It is well worth your time to craft an outline of a pitch that you can use in different situations. Your pitch can be part of your visual resume too. It could be condensed and used as a headline to capture the reader's attention.

Key Components to Gather

As mentioned in Chapter 2, there are certain elements you will need as you begin creating your resume, social profiles, and maybe even your own website. When you have all these things ready to go, it will speed up the process, and more importantly, your message will be consistent no matter where you are sharing it.

Headshot

A professional photograph is a must-have in today's socially connected world. It is used on your web page, social network profiles, maybe even your business card.

The All-Important, Yet Dreaded, Headshot

There have been claims that social profiles with a real photo, not an avatar, blank space, or logo, are more likely to be clicked and viewed than those without a photo. Yet historically, HR has not wanted to see photos on resumes for fear it might be accused of discrimination. You should carefully consider the advantages and disadvantages of using a photo on your resume. However, when creating social profiles and on your website, a headshot is a must!

Michael Hyatt, author of a *New York Times* bestseller, *Platform: Get Noticed in a Noisy World*, and former chairman and CEO of Thomas Nelson Publishers, focuses his attention on helping leaders leverage their influence. From his experience in the publishing world and his involvement in social media, Michael makes these recommendations for getting the best possible headshot.

"The right photo can help establish credibility, build trust, and promote engagement. These are at the heart of connecting in the world of social media and essential if you ever hope to sell someone on what you have to offer," states Michael.[4]

The goal is to capture the genuine, real-deal you, not a facade or someone you desire to be. Here are some of Michael's suggestions for getting the right headshot:

- **Invest in a professional photographer.** The results will impress, and you only have one chance to make a good first impression. The quality and the design of the photograph absolutely make a difference. Professional photographers usually take hundreds of shots, which ensures that there will be at least a couple that will work.

39

- **Find a unique backdrop.** While it is common to want a background that is neutral, consider the advantage you would have if you were to select a special background, such as your favorite building, garden, or other location. You are trying to create interest without being overly distracting.
- **Dress the part.** Wear clothes that fit the type of role you are pursuing. Choose the appropriate colors for your skin and hair color as well. Bringing several outfits will give you options in case you change your mind down the road.
- **Smile and look at the camera.** The best smile is one that uses your whole face, including the eyes. And be sure you look directly at the camera lens.
- **Remember that a headshot is a shot of your head.** You want to make sure that the photo shows your head, not your whole body. Make sure the photographer zooms in.

These are recommendations. If you choose not to embrace any or all of these recommendations, do so with purpose and intent.

Bio or Summary

A short and longer version of who you are, what you've accomplished, and what your goals are helps tell your overall story.

Your Summary and Bio

Both your summary and bio provide a high-level overview of your background. What they are attempting to do is summarize your story. The difference between the two lies in the length of time you have, your audience's needs, and your situation. While every version can include similar key phrases to emphasize important elements, each is delivered differently based on who will read it and how.

Good writers realize that writing is a series of drafts and edits. Pull the information together for now and go back and edit later.

By answering those questions and creating a worksheet, you can then pick and choose the most important, interesting, and relevant information to include when you tell your story. The summary or bio appears in many places as you manage your message.

The Summary on Your Resume

The general recommendation is to include a summary on your resume. You may just use keywords, or you may put together a short paragraph; either way, the words need to convey why you are qualified and capable of performing the work you are pursuing. Based on the job requirements, you may have to fine-tune your summary to include the right words, as long as you do not lie, exaggerate, or stretch the truth. In Chapter 4, you'll see an example of a professionally crafted resume summary.

Your LinkedIn Summary

Your LinkedIn summary is more robust, thorough, and comprehensive than your resume summary, especially if you are interested in different types of jobs. LinkedIn defines your summary as "information about your mission, accomplishments, and goals." Your summary can contain up to 2,000 characters, so don't worry about not having enough space to tell your story. Chapter 8 contains examples of LinkedIn profiles, including summaries, to help inspire you.

Your Bio

Shorter in length than your summary, your bio should capture the most important pieces of information for your intended audience. Your bio is requested on many social networking sites and community profiles and is needed for speaking engagements and article submissions, as well as being an important component of your career marketing materials. Think about the short 160 characters Twitter and Pinterest showcase your bio. Make your bio memorable by including information unique to you, such as specific skills, interests, and hobbies. Luckily, the social network Google+ provides almost unlimited characters to highlight your best assets. You can see some examples later in this chapter.

Your Value Proposition

There is one more piece to perfect before moving on. The information you've been cataloging is important to you; however, it may not necessarily mean as much to your audience. It is up to you to connect the dots about the value you can deliver. Your value proposition puts your value in terms that are meaningful to your audience and others. In order to do this, you have to understand what your readers' problems are and how you can solve them. Start by answering three questions:

- What problem do you solve? (Look at your projects and accomplishments.)
- How do you do it uniquely? (Look at your personality traits.)
- Whom do you do it for? (Check your list of industries or types of projects.)

Kristen Roberts, a graphic designer featured in the next chapter, uses this personal statement: "A talented artist turned designer with a passion for creating effective visual communications, I strive to turn dreams into reality while exceeding employer and client expectations."

Resume

A traditional text version of your resume is still important. Many applicant tracking systems and hiring professionals still want to see this. Your portfolio can contain both a visual and text version of your resume.

Your Resume

Yes, this book is about visual resumes; however, you will need to have a text version available as well. Many third-party recruiters, contracted by employers to screen and recommend candidates, rely heavily on the traditional resume format. It is search-friendly and familiar, and they can find what they are looking for easily.

Social Media Outlet Links

When you include links to these channels, you provide greater insight into your communication style, interests, and personality. The links also demonstrate your expertise. In addition, they provide evidence that you are technically savvy.

Social Media Outlets

Having a presence on social media outlets provides you with the opportunity to demonstrate what you know, shows you are up on current trends and technology, and can prove your communication skills. More importantly, as you will discover throughout this book, employers are searching online through social networks and also are building what they call talent communities of potential hires through Facebook, Twitter, and LinkedIn. These outlets allow you to have more interaction with potential employers and increase their awareness of you.

Most Popular Social Networks

There are many social networks, and each has unique benefits. The four networks mentioned were selected because of their large user bases and the fact that employers have begun establishing accounts on them to recruit talent. You will personally benefit from using these social networks because they increase your online presence.

- LinkedIn. Known as the go-to social network for professionals, LinkedIn is a must for anyone. This is a closed network, and therefore you need to have connections with people in order to communicate with them. For more on creating a robust and eye-catching LinkedIn profile, see Chapter 8.
- Facebook. Though it's primarily a collection of friends, family, and personal relationships, you will notice more corporations, businesses, and organizations developing pages and groups where they talk about their culture, events, and other news.
- Twitter. Users send and read tweets, which are text messages limited to 140 characters. You can follow anyone and anyone can follow you, which makes this an open network.
- Google+. The wide array of topics and users makes this a great network to explore. Like Twitter, this is an open network that allows you to message or reference any user in your updates.

43

And as a Google product, this can only help with your online visibility.

Claim Your Profiles Across Social Media Outlets

Do you have a profile on Twitter, Facebook, Flickr, YouTube, or SlideShare? You can see if your name is available by checking out hundreds of social networking sites; try using namechk.com or knowem.com.

Increase your digital footprint by claiming a profile on multiple sites. This is the beginning of the "build and share" part of your message, and it will be addressed throughout the book.

- Twitter bio (see Figure 3-1)

FIGURE 3-1
Award-Winning Fun Writer
http://bit.ly/1b06stL

- Pinterest bio (see Figure 3-2)

FIGURE 3-2
Infographics Expert and Geek
http://bit.ly/1altXk5

- Google+ bio (see Figure 3-3)

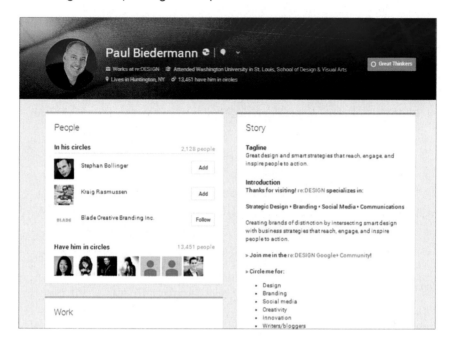

FIGURE 3-3
Smart and Engaging Marketer
http://bit.ly/1eGDqnE

Tools for Hosting and Sharing Files

The following social tools are important for sharing your story. You need not be a master of them all; however, you should at least know what they do and how they can help market your message.

These next three sites integrate with LinkedIn, which allows you to easily add work samples to your LinkedIn profile:

- **Behance.** A portfolio of your work created on Behance will easily be shared across the web. You need not be a designer to benefit from using Behance to show samples of work.
- **Box.** A file sharing and collaborative site allows you to upload documents and easily access them from any computer anywhere.
- **SlideShare.** Presentations and documents are uploaded and shared.

45

The following sites are media-sharing sites:

- Flickr. Users upload photographs and short videos, making it easier to share to other social networking sites. It is also one of the more popular destinations people turn to in order to find images.
- Instagram. This network is designed to share photos and images with people following your account and cross-share to other social media accounts.
- Pinterest. Users pin images or pictures that are shared and added to boards. It functions like an online scrapbook.
- SoundCloud. People use this social network for collecting and sharing music or audio files.
- Tumblr. Users easily post multimedia content to a short-form blog. Users can allow anyone to follow their blogs or choose to keep blogs private.
- YouTube. This is the most popular video-hosting site. Users upload and share videos to other social media channels and websites.

Portfolio of Work

Many occupations ask for work samples today. Whether you have your own website that houses your work or you have links to other creative portfolio sites, having digital and easily shareable work will eliminate hours searching for the best samples later on when you need to find them. Your digital content is also searchable online, which means someone may stumble upon it in a search for a potential future employee with your talent.

Consistency

The information you include in your profiles, bios, or resumes—or anywhere else you summarize who you are and what you do—has to be consistent. Take a step back; even ask trusted friends or colleagues for their advice. Make sure the message you use captures the most relevant, important, and marketable assets you want to showcase.

If you want to chart a course that differentiates you from other professionals in the same marketplace, the first step is being able to complete the sentence, "A company hires me over other professionals because . . ." How are you first, only, faster, better or cheaper than other people who want to do what you're doing in the world?[5]

—REID HOFFMAN, cofounder of LinkedIn

CHAPTER 4

Resumes with Visual Flair

It isn't enough to have a pretty resume. It has to deliver results. It is also important to have a plain-text version available as well. A traditional Word document resume will likely be required when submitting an online job application through an applicant tracking system (ATS). In these circumstances, you will want to make sure your resume contains the requisite information. The elements of a "good" resume can vary by industry or occupation, and this chapter will take a look at what to you can do to make your qualifications pop and your visual resume attract attention.

> It's a highly competitive job market and you have to clearly demonstrate how your unique skills and experience are relevant and beneficial to that particular employer. We see more people using infographics, QR codes and visual resumes to package their information in new and interesting ways.
>
> —**ROSEMARY HAEFNER,** Vice President of Human Resources at CareerBuilder[1]

Making the Initial Cut

There are certain pieces of information that employers look for when skimming a resume. How long they actually review a resume depends on the personal preferences of the reviewer. Six seconds is the average amount of time reviewers give to a first review of a resume, according to study by TheLadders.[2] In a CareerBuilder study, one in five HR managers reported that they spend less than 30 seconds reviewing applications, and around 40 percent spend less than one minute, according to Rosemary Haefner. Whether it is 6 or 30 seconds, neither is long enough to digest the vast amounts of information you've so carefully selected to go on your resume. You can follow some of these best practices to help your resume make it to the next round:

1. The overall layout should be visually appealing. Allow for enough white space and sufficient margins so the written information is readable.

2 The heading should contain vital information such as your name and how to contact you. The heading is also a good place to put your web address or LinkedIn profile URL. If space allows, you may want to include a link to your visual, infographic, or social resume as well.

3. Your summary answers these questions: "What makes you unique?" and "Why should I hire you?"

4. Technical skills might include the specific instrumentation or lab equipment that you use. It might also contain a list of the hardware, operating systems, or software that you've experienced, especially if you are an IT professional.

5. Your work experience should flow from the most recent to the oldest and clearly define your employer and job title for each position you mention.

6. Your job title should be meaningful to people outside your company. For example, if you had an unusual title, which seems to be in fashion these days, you may also need to include the more commonly recognized title—for instance, Chief Catalyst/ Marketing Manager. If your title is too vague, you should add clarification by specifying the department, division, or specialty you practiced—Analyst/Business Process Research.

7. Anyone looking at your resume wants to know for each job how long you worked there and when you worked there. You don't need to include exact dates on your resume; however, you should provide them on the job application.

8. Instead of just listing common job duties, take it a step further and accentuate achievements, including the positive outcomes of your work.

9. Education and professional development are important, but seldom as important as the experience you gained from doing the job. List the schools you attended and the degree you received or pursued. Including a graduation date may not be necessary if it was more than 5 to 10 years ago.

10. Certifications, publications, licenses, community activities, and professional associations should be included as long as they are relevant or serve a purpose on your resume.

It is difficult to provide concrete terms or suggestions given the wide range of people and ATSs used to evaluate your resume. Sadly, if you ask 10 people for feedback on your resume, you are likely to receive 10 different recommendations. (See Figure 4-1.)

①

NAME
Street Address
City, State Zip
Telephone number
Email Address
LinkedIn URL

②

SUMMARY OF QUALIFCATIONS

③ *The summary is a concise statement summarizing experience, areas of expertise, technical or professional skills, traits and any distinctions. It is very closely linked to your Positioning Statement or Elevator Pitch.*
Profession/Job Title with extensive experience in the _____ industry. Area of expertise in _____ and _____. Strengths include:

- ____   - ____
- ____   - ____

④

TECHNICAL SKILLS
(If appropriate)

PROFESSIONAL EXPERIENCE

⑤ EMPLOYER**,** City, State
⑥ **Job Title**   **200X - 200X** ⑦
[Briefly describe scope of work or short job description]

⑧
  ▪ Accomplishment (Action + Result) Quantify or qualify
  ▪ Accomplishment (Action + Result) Quantify or qualify
  ▪ Accomplishment (Action + Result) Quantify or qualify

EMPLOYER, City, State   **200X – 200X**
Job Title
[Briefly describe scope of work or short job description]

  ▪ Accomplishment (Action + Result) Quantify or qualify
  ▪ Accomplishment (Action + Result) Quantify or qualify
  ▪ Accomplishment (Action + Result) Quantify or qualify

EMPLOYER, City, State   **19XX – 19XX**
Job Title
[Briefly scope of work or short job description]
  ▪ Fewer bullets the further back you go, emphasis should be on current skills

⑨   ### EDUCATION AND PROFESSIONAL DEVELOPMENT
DEGREE, School, City State   Graduation Date

⑩   **LICENSES** (or) **CERTIFICATIONS**
[License/certification] , "[School or Organization Issued]"

MILITARY SERVICE
"[Branch of Service, Highest Rank, Special training, Honorable Discharge]"

AWARDS
"[Name of Award and what it was for, Company/Organization]"

LANGUAGES
"[Spanish, French, Other?]"

VOLUNTEER WORK (or) **COMMUNITY ACTIVITIES**
"[Title or Function, Name of Organization]"

FIGURE 4-1 **Resume Format**

Does Your Resume Answer These Questions?

The overall purpose of the resume is to convince the reader to contact you. The job posting usually provides a good list of skills and keywords for you to reference in your resume. Every resume you submit should answer these three questions for the reader:

- Can you do the job?
- Will you do the job?
- Will I like working with you?

Test Your Resume

With so many different preferences and styles of resumes, deciding which to use and which will be most successful in securing an interview should be based on how well you meet the reviewer's preferences and qualifications for the job. Try asking yourself these questions before you radically change your resume or decide to implement changes:

- Does it address the audience (employer's) needs?
  - Do you show you meet the qualifications and requirements of the job?
- How will it be consumed?
  - Digitally or paper?
- Is it unique?
- Does it convey personality?
  - Do your values, work ethic, and priorities come out?
- Does it demonstrate expertise?
  - Does it tell more than the duties you performed?
  - Does it show the level of responsibility you can hold or initiative you have taken?
- Is it clear?
  - Will the reader know what you are talking about, or have you used jargon or terms the reader may not be familiar with?
- Is your contact information readily available?

- Do you link to other online resources (portfolio, social network profiles)?
- Is it visually appealing?
  - Does it contain consistent design elements (font, use of space, etc.)
- Will it compel the reader to take action?
- Have you followed the submission instructions for the job?

Creative Success Stories

CareerBuilder released the results of a study of the most creative techniques that worked in 2012. The study asked 2,298 hiring managers nationwide what they liked and what they didn't like about resumes they'd received. Maybe some of these real-life examples will help jump-start your creativity:[3]

- Candidate sent his resume in the form of an oversized Rubik's Cube, where you had to push the tiles around to align the resume. He was hired.
- Candidate who had been a stay-at-home mom listed her skills as nursing, housekeeping, chef, teacher, biohazard cleanup, fight referee, taxi driver, secretary, tailor, personal shopping assistant, and therapist. She was hired.
- Candidate created a marketing brochure promoting herself as the best candidate and was hired.
- Candidate applying for a food and beverage management position sent a resume in the form of a fine-dining menu and was hired.
- Candidate crafted his resume to look like Google search results for the "perfect candidate." Candidate ultimately wasn't hired but was considered.

The Most Common Pitfalls to Avoid

It should be obvious, but no matter what your occupation or what type of resume you are using, avoid these blunders that will automatically dismiss a candidate from consideration:

55

- Typos
- Inappropriate e-mail address
- Large amounts of wording from the job posting
- Blocks of text with little white space

Learn from Graphic Designers

The trend toward more creative resumes is prominent among graphic designers. This makes sense. Their resumes serve as a sample of their work. A resume created by a graphic designer is visual proof of his or her design knowledge and skills.

But the growing trend toward graphic-styled resumes is occurring in noncreative occupations and industries. The reasons? Visual resumes will stand out. Visual aids were found to be 43 percent more persuasive than other forms of presentation materials.[4] And urban legend tells us that visuals are *processed 60,000* times *faster* than text, which appeals to busy, overworked resume reviewers.

Visual Resumes

Typography is the art of using font to convey your message. Many of the resumes you'll see were created in a graphic design program like InDesign. Without some design experience, it may be beyond your reach to create a resume that looks as good as these. However, if you visit graphic designer sites like Dribbble, Deviant Art, or Behance, you can search for graphic designers who specialize in creating these types of resumes.

Why This Works

Kelly Weihs's resume oozes creative. Her use of design elements such as color, lines, type, and texture blend well to show off her work. Not any style would have worked for Kelly. Her love of history heavily influenced her design choice. This helps blend her interests with her skills and talents for a meaningful message. (See Figure 4-2.)

JW Design & Illustration

kellyweihs.com
kelly.weihs@gmail.com
Baltimore, Maryland

 THE OBJECTIVE
To create.

INVALUABLE ASSETS!

Outgoing friendly person, driven by a strong work ethic, multi-tasker, organized, detail oriented

* Confident with Adobe Photoshop, Adobe Illustrator,
* Adobe InDesign, MAC and PC, digital drawing tablet,
* inkjet printers, scanners, digital cameras and
* always eager to learn new software skills.

★WORK EXPERIENCE★

DIAMOND SELECT TOYS
Graphic Designer, Timonium, MD
MAY 2011 - CURRENT
Design toy packaging, print advertisements, online promotions, trade show materials, photograph products.

CRAYOLA Intern
Easton, PA
MARCH - MAY 2010
Assisted designers with packaging comps and presentation materials and designed promotions.

EDUCATION

BFA in Communication Design with Concentrations in Illustration & Graphic Design
Kutztown University of Pennsylvania, Kutztown, PA, May 2010
GPA in major: 3.83

ACTIVITIES & INTERESTS

Designathon, Volunteer, Spring 2010
House Industries' Monogram Workshop, Spring 2010
Ilene Strizver Gourmet Typography Workshop, Spring 2009
American Institute of Graphic Arts, Member, 2008–2013

* VOLUNTEER DESIGNER
* Jerusalem Mill Village, Kingsville, MD
* AUG 2011–Current (Seasonal)
* Designed event programs and flyers

WORK FOR HIRE ★ HONORS

Sales Associate, Plow & Hearth, Hunt Valley, MD Aug. 2010–Apr.2012
Managed 'key items', created signs highlighting sales, assisted customers with purchasing decisions.

Sales Associate, Kohl's, Bel Air, MD May–August 2008
Friendly sales associate and cashier always prepared to help any customer

Terry Boyle Spring 2010
Illustration Award

DEAN'S LIST
Fall 2008 – Spring 2010

FIGURE 4-2 **Typography Graphic Designer** http://bit.ly/1mOKKhd

Why This Works

Though technically, this next resume might be categorized as an infographic resume, it is used here as an example of how typeface and layout work together to craft a visual resume. Kristen Roberts's personal statement sets the tone for her resume and shows her focus on the needs of the employer while also showcasing her commitment to her occupation. (See Figure 4-3.)

kristen ROBERTS
GRAPHIC DESIGNER

☎ ██████████
✉ hello@kristen-victoria.com

EDUCATION

Associate's Degree
GRAPHIC + WEB DESIGN
EAGLE GATE COLLEGE · 2010 - 2012

EXPERIENCE

2.5 years
FREELANCE

PROJECTS + SKILLS

Print Design
Blog Design
Brand Identity
Art/Illustration
Photo Editing

WHAT I USE MOST

PHOTOSHOP
Illustrator
InDesign
CSS / HTML

ADDITIONAL TECH SKILLS:
Microsoft Office, Mac, PC,
Blogger, Facebook, Twitter

PERSONAL STATEMENT

" A talented artist turned designer with a passion for creating effective visual communications, I strive to turn dreams into reality while exceeding employer and client expectations. "

EMPLOYMENT HISTORY

(references available upon request)

6/2011 - PRESENT — *Kv's Design Studio - Freelance*
Available for a variety of projects ranging from logos and business cards to wedding invitations and blog designs.

2/2012 - PRESENT — *Reardon Real Estate - Transaction Coordinator*
Assisting a real estate team consisting of two agents, I operate all administrative needs, organize schedules and tasks, increase social media engagement, while helping successfully close an estimated 40-60 yearly transactions.

12/2010 - 12/2011 — *Ferrari Color - Customer Communications*
Assisted clients, directed calls, managed mail and filing system, provided help desk service for Sports Illustrated and TIME Cover cutomers, while gaining a knowledge of the print industry.

10/2009 - 10/2010 — *The Woods on Ninth - Administrative Assistant*
Assisted the Director of Operations with managing employees and ensuring successful events. Created all advertisements and managed company website, created an effective filing system, gained knowledge of business and management.

THINGS I ENJOY

Coffee   Blogging   Photography   Fashion   Drawing   Travel   Typography

PORTFOLIO   KRISTENVICTORIA.CARBONMADE.COM

FIGURE 4-3 **Typography Makes a Statement** http://bit.ly/UVzERO

Why This Works

Adrienne Robenstine's orange graphic designer resume makes a stand-out example. He clearly states his occupation and summarizes immediately, under his title, his key qualifications and attributes. He also lists valuable technical skills within his industry and shows professional organizations he is affiliated with. A QR code at the bottom helps emphasize his familiarity with current technology trends. (See Figure 4-4.)

adrienne robenstine
GRAPHIC DESIGNER • MARKETER • CREATIVE VIRTUOSO

123.456.7890
a.robenstine@gmail.com

I AM A GRAPHIC DESIGNER

Pre-press, digital and offset print production.
Web design, creation, maintenance and flash animation.
Deadline driven and oriented.
Comfortable working in high pressure situations.
Cohesive brand identity and logo creation.
Innovative and on the cutting edge of technology.
Extensive marketing budget management.

EDUCATION

The University of Akron
Class of 2007

Major: Graphic Design
Minor: Professional Photography & Marketing

MEMBERSHIPS
NAPP • AIGA • CDPUG

COMPUTER KNOWLEDGE

Proficient in both Mac and Windows operating systems.

SOFTWARE

Adobe
Acrobat
After Effects CS6
Dreamweaver CS6
Flash CS6
Illustrator CS6
InDesign CS6
Photoshop CS6
Premiere Pro CS6

Quark
QuarkXpress

Microsoft
Excel
Powerpoint
Word

PROFESSIONAL EXPERIENCE

SELF EMPLOYED *Geneva, Ohio*
Graphic Designer, Marketing Professional, Photographer

2007-Present Worked various projects including logo design and reconstruction, business cards, brochures, wedding invitations, direct mail pieces and postcards. I have worked with such clients as Wente Vineyards of California, The Q Arena, Heidelberg Distributing Company and many others. Helped develop cohesive marketing plans to increase business and revenue.

MONT GRANITE, INC. *Solon, Ohio*
Marketing Director & Graphic Designer

2010-2011 I handled the marketing efforts and graphic design for their 5 different locations. I created a company wide cohesive brand appearance, designed and maintained all internal print publications as well as creating ads and advertising in several publications. I designed a 10' x 10' tradeshow booth and organized and presented at several tradeshows in all of their markets. Researched new technology and applied social media marketing to all divisions. Instilled QR Code marketing into all print ads as well as on all employee business cards. Created a state of the art website including an extensive material search and database. Developed an industry first way of scanning granite slabs to reproduce material for homeowners to look at in their home.

PIP PRINTING & MARKETING SERVICES *Mentor, Ohio*
Art Director / Graphic Designer

2008-2010 Worked as the head of the Graphics Department. Designed all pieces as well as running pre-press and production. Designed a variety of pieces ranging from Business Cards, Brochures, Menus, Postcards, Catalogs, Direct Mail pieces, etc. I created an archival system for client files and ran server back up for secure file storage. I created, edited and laid out as well as editing and manipulating photographs for full color 150 page book by a local author. Instilled and maintained social media marketing.

PORATH PRINT SOURCE *Cleveland, Ohio*
Graphic Designer

2007-2008 Worked with several high level clientele such as local radio stations and charitable organizations. Created unique designs for business cards, brochures, calendars and direct mail pieces. Prepared files for digital and 4-color print production including outputing color plates and running color tests. Gained valuable experience in pre-press machinery. Maintained file archival and storage.

PORTFOLIO AND REFERENCES AVAILABLE UPON REQUEST

SCAN ME

FIGURE 4-4 **Creative Virtuoso Pops with Orange** http://bit.ly/L82utj

Why This Works

Kyle Bahr has a diverse set of interests as evidenced by his headline. His personal statement also helps the reader see his strengths in communication. Kyle's resume teeters on the edge of being an infographic with it subtle icon art and graphs. (See Figure 4-5.)

KYLE BAHR

DIGITAL STRATEGIST | WILDERNESS EXPLORER | GENTLEMAN

I'm a creator of content, a shaper of ideas, a risk taker and a collaborator. I believe a message stands a much better chance of being remembered if it tickles the senses. If it has a soul. And that's what I do.

✏ PROFESSIONAL EXPERIENCE

SENIOR CONTENT STRATEGIST / Growthweaver, Denver, CO
Using fewer words and more voice, I connected with today's overly stimulated consumer using social posts that doubled as paid ads. I produced clever, relevant content at lightning speeds—content that people actually read, and responded to—creating more transparent, profitable, responsive, likable companies. In fact, a client once called my work their "gold standard."

SOCIAL MEDIA STRATEGIST / Creative Marketing Partners, Miami, FL
Applied my writing skills to stimulate conversations that helped make sense of the universe. Then, extended that insight into powerful engagement strategies, synthesizing and integrating social media and digital content. Also prepared measurement and impact reports summarizing the results of social media campaigns.

NEW MEDIA EDITOR + WRITER / Sprout, Minneapolis, MN
Going green should be easy. That was the idea driving our start-up company Sprout. Two months after its launch, 1,300 Sprouters had joined the site. Four months after its launch, Sprout listed 550 local merchants offering green products or services. I wrote web articles, collateral, video scripts, social media updates, and a wide variety of other content, driving cohesive editorial themes. Not to mention, I worked closely with the CEO to improve the thinking, direction of the strategy, and recommended programs and tactics.

SALES & MARKETING ASSOCIATE / Arkansas Valley Adventures, Breckenridge, CO
Managed leads through the full sales cycle from introductory calls to closing deals. Generated more than $35,000 in revenue in three months. Suggested and optimized tactics for digital programs.

✷ SKILL SETS & QUALITIES

DIGITAL SKILLS

Social Media Marketing	PPC/Facebook Ads
Digital Sales	Photoshop
Analytics	Coda/Dreamweaver
Blogging	HTML5 & CSS3

PERSONAL QUALITIES

Empathy	Smiling
Charisma	Integrity
Storytelling	Attention Span
Luck	Ego

⚑ EDUCATION

UNIVERSITY OF MINNESOTA
Bachelor of Science in Sport Marketing, Emphasis in Entrepreneurship

⤴ RESULTS (click me)

Argonaut Wine & Liquor
Sprout
American Furniture Warehouse
High Plains Library District

♥ HOBBIES

Poker   Meditation   The Packers   Exploring   Snowboarding

⚊ CONTACT

☏
✉ hey@kylebahr.com
🖥 kylebahr.com

FIGURE 4-5 **Digital Strategist** http://bit.ly/1m0Zm1e

Steve Retka's visual resume succinctly highlights his most marketable qualifications—past experience, familiarity with popular social tools, and key skills. The contrast in colors, use of space, and typeface all work together to convey a cohesive message. He uses a very simple timeline to show work experience, and he uses symbols of social media tools and more images along with words at the bottom of the page to present his specific skills. (See Figure 4-6.)

Putting Your Toe in the Graphic Water

More conservative industries and occupations may not be ready for a full-fledged infographic resume. Master resume writer Jacqui Barrett-Poindexter talks about how just one graphic on a resume can set it apart and powerfully showcase a key accomplishment:

> Charts, graphs and tables add value to resume stories by providing a glimpse-able view of a crucial achievement or series of achievements. In this example, a profit transformation that the candidate spearheaded is snapshotted to quickly show the reader that this person can take floundering bottom-lines and turn them around in short order (just one year). Specifically, this Profit Turnaround bar graph tells the story of a 5-quarter profit turnaround, converting an $11 million quarterly loss to quarterly profit of $8.3 million
>
> Since "individuals" read resumes, and each reader (hiring decision maker, recruiter, human resource professional, or networking contact) has his or her unique way of processing information, it makes sense to provide both words and pictures to illustrate a candidate's value. What works for one reader may not work for the next, so offering options is ideal.
>
> As well, I have found for my clients, adding illustrations and images that pop deepens and adds dimension to their storyboard resume. These clients are attracting attention and

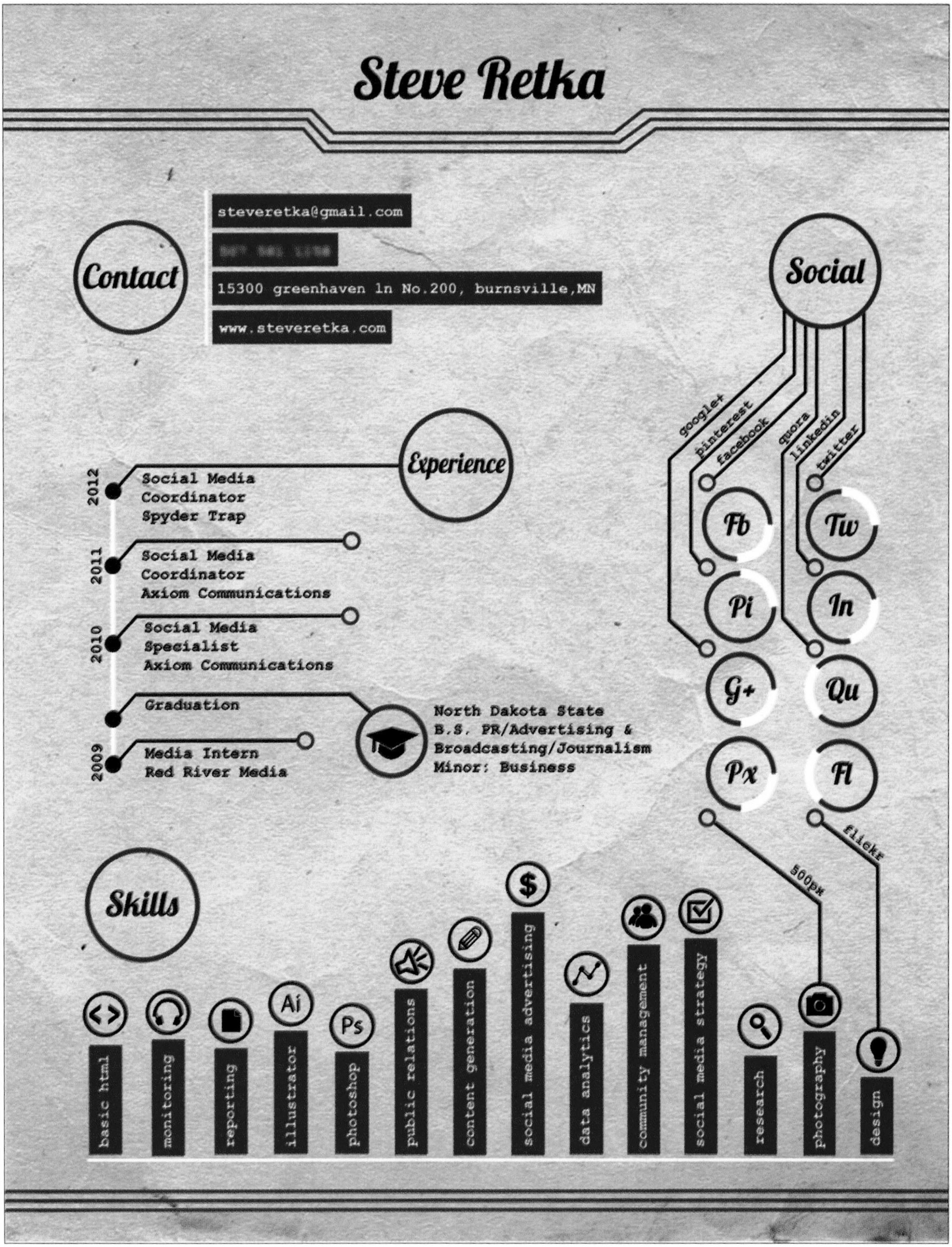

Steve Retka

Contact

steveretka@gmail.com

▮▮▮ ▮▮▮ ▮▮▮▮

15300 greenhaven ln No.200, burnsville,MN

www.steveretka.com

Social

googlet
pinterest
facebook
quora
linkedin
twitter

Fb
Tw
Pi
In
G+
Qu
Px
Fl

500px
flickr

Experience

2012 Social Media
Coordinator
Spyder Trap

2011 Social Media
Coordinator
Axiom Communications

2010 Social Media
Specialist
Axiom Communications

Graduation
North Dakota State
B.S. PR/Advertising &
Broadcasting/Journalism
Minor: Business

2009 Media Intern
Red River Media

Skills

basic html
monitoring
reporting
illustrator
photoshop
public relations
content generation
social media advertising
data analytics
community management
social media strategy
research
photography
design

FIGURE 4-6 **Social Media Coordinator** http://bit.ly/1kWSfpk

driving more traffic to their resume by having the courage to sell their value versus reining in their marketing message.

Finally, in some instances, what might take a larger bundle of words to articulate can sometimes be explained, with flair, in a smaller, more pithy visual space occupied by a chart or graph.

The caveat is not to force the idea of illustrating your resume with images, but to intuitively knit them into the fabric as you see fit and as makes sense to the target reader.

You can learn more about Jacqui's work as a forward-thinking, master-level career writer, on her site careertrend.net. (See Figure 4-7.)

Totally Out of the Box

There are times when something completely out of the ordinary captures attention and spreads virally. With what is known as the Amazon-style resume, Philippe Dubost captured the attention of millions in early 2013, literally. Philippe reported on his blog that after just three weeks his resume netted these impressive numbers:[5]

- **1.3M** unique visitors, from **219 countries** (reached 1M on Feb 1st, after only 8 days)
- **39,000** Facebook likes
- **1,100** e-mails received
- **800** LinkedIn connection requests
- **2,149** Twitter mentions (and thousands of related tweets; haven't found a reliable way to count them yet)
- **704** different referring domains

But the most important statistic of all—he landed a job.

FIRST NAME LASTNAME

Address
City, State Zip

email | LinkedIn URL

Home: 555.555.4321
Cell: 555.555.1234

CHIEF EXECUTIVE OFFICER (CEO)

BUSINESS AND CULTURE TRANSFORMATION | HIGH GROWTH / PROFIT | STARTUP MANAGEMENT

Display Executive Toughness as a really-gets-things-done guy. Strong sense of urgency in relentless pursuit of priorities. Strategize and implement large-scale change programs within operations.

EXECUTIVE VALUE SNAPSHOT

Entrepreneurial-spirited executive and **catalyst for exponential growth** with progressive leadership in the oil, gas and pipeline industries. Financially astute strategist and planner who has led crucial business growth initiatives, including business unit turnarounds, M&A strategies and business integrations.

Robust team builder and leader with **strong P&L, operational and commercial focus.** Integrate people, processes and technology to drive dramatic and positive organizational change. Dismantle barriers, mend bridges and align operations, commercial and engineering to collaborate on common goals. Solid academic credentials that include an MBA in Finance and Strategy.

➔ **Operations Revamp:** Restructured 157-year-old pipeline company, initiating culture change to focus on profit / safety. Streamlined staffing 32%; boosted operating results; and cut incidents 80%.

➔ **Acquisition Integration:** Led more than $3B in new acquisitions in 18 months, affecting 12% revenue growth and 19% EBITDA increase, concurrent with headcount operating expense reduction.

➔ **Business Unit Transformation:** Turned around two failing business units, introducing new processes and discipline. Revenue escalated by $32M for one unit; EBITDA grew by 59% at the other, within one year.

➔ **Strategy and Direction:** Refocused business unit on customer needs; drove 38% EBITDA improvement.

➔ **Compliance:** Assumed compliance of company that was failing audits and under a federal consent decree. Developed action plans; influenced teams; decree was lifted and all audit deliverables met.

LEADERSHIP PROGRESSION

COMPANY NAME [WWW.COMPANYNAME.COM, NYSE: COM], City, State, 2008 to Present
Company detail.

President of 3 Business Units *(2011 to Present)* Promoted to lead the turnaround of two foundering business units and one strong unit that was lacking a clear customer focus. **Concurrently serve as the President of all three businesses,** replacing three former executive colleagues. Hold direct P&L accountability for the development and implementation of strategies to enhance operational efficiency, commercial development and improve profitability for the following business units:

Business One: Develop and execute strategies to improve business efficiency, reduce costs and hedge against risk of severe market backwardation for this $4 billion trading / marketing organization, with 30 employees, selling refined product to 45 markets in the Northeast and Midwest.

Leadership Impact: Captained a mission and vision **focus on profitability.** Engineered a **>$22 million turnaround** in one year, shifting unit from quarterly loss of ($11 million) to $8.3 million profit in Q4 2011.

Headcount decreased by 50%, working capital by two-thirds, inventories by one-half while implementing effective hedging strategies.

Profit Turnaround

FIGURE 4-7 **Standard Resume with Graph**

Why This Works

Unique, creative, easy to share, and luck. These were the things that made Dubost's resume work. It will be hard for someone to duplicate this stunt, but it should spark some creative juices and help you think beyond traditional. (See Figure 4-8.)

FIGURE 4-8
**Amazonlike
Resume**
http://bit.ly/1d0SllJ

What Won't Work

Creativity has to be used on the right audience. Perhaps well intentioned, or perhaps not, these are some examples that didn't catch the right type of attention from the audience. In a survey by CareerBuilder,[6] hiring managers shared the most memorable, unusual, and inadvisable applications that came across their desk:

- Candidate called himself a genius and invited the hiring manager to interview him at his apartment.
- Candidate's cover letter talked about her family being in the mob.
- Candidate applying for a management job listed "gator hunting" as a skill.
- Candidate's resume included phishing as a hobby.
- Candidate specified that her resume was set up to be sung to the tune of "The Brady Bunch."
- Candidate highlighted the fact that he was "Homecoming Prom Prince" in 1984.

68

- Candidate claimed to be able to speak "Antarctican" when applying for a job to work in Antarctica.
- Candidate's resume had a photo of the applicant reclining in a hammock under the headline "Hi, I'm _____ and I'm looking for a job."
- Candidate's resume was decorated with pink rabbits.
- Candidate listed "to make dough" as the objective on the resume.
- Candidate applying for an accounting job said he was "dee-tail-oriented" and spelled the company's name incorrectly.
- Candidate's cover letter contained "LOL."

Words of Caution

If you decide you are going to use a visual resume, or an infographic resume like the ones you'll see in the next chapter, you need to evaluate your resume's results. In other words, is your phone ringing? Put your marketing hat on. As with any marketing campaign, the proof is in outcomes generated—in this case, calls. If your phone isn't ringing, then your resume isn't working. Chapter 12 will also help you discover ways to measure and assess how many people are viewing and sharing your material, but the best indicator is the number of people who contact you for the right types of potential job opportunities.

CHAPTER 5

Infographic Resumes

The earliest forms of communication were pictographs painted on cave walls, advancing to Egyptian hieroglyphics, and finally to the alphabet and printing press, which exponentially spread the written language. It's been hypothesized that our brains can process pictures faster than words. The classic example that is used to prove this point is a picture of a circle versus the words "a curved line with every line equidistant from the center." Today we are bombarded with data, facts, and information. Our language has grown from 207,930 words during Shakespeare's time to over 469,470 in modern times.[1] Perhaps this complexity is why our primitive brain craves the simplicity of communication through pictures. Add to this the shrinking adult attention span. Experts suggest the average attention span has decreased from 12 minutes to 5 minutes in the past decade.[2] Perhaps further contributing to the desire for images over text is the rapid growth in the use of mobile devices. Have you tried reading large quantities of text from your smartphone? It's not surprising, given the circumstances, that search volume for infographics has risen over 800 percent in the last few years, according to HubSpot, an inbound marketing company.[3] So, is the age-old saying "A picture is worth a thousand words" more relevant today than ever?

A poll conducted by Beyond.com, an online career network to connect job seekers and employers, found that over 57 percent of the HR professionals polled said that an infographic or visual-style resume would help them more quickly evaluate candidates over a traditional resume.[4]

Data Visualization

Infographics take complex data or information and put it in pictures or diagrams to make it easier to comprehend. To create an infographic, you start with data and transform it into easily digestible images. Take, for example, the use of pie charts and bar charts to convey sales numbers or company profits in order for the shareholders to understand. Typically, data, in its raw form, can overwhelm or confuse an audience. Creating a visual representation of what the data really means is the power and beauty of infographics.

Though you are far from being able to submit an infographic instead of a text resume to apply for a job, it is an eye-catching alternative to the overwhelming look of a page cluttered with words. Your infographic resume serves as an alternative or supplemental communication piece. Consider showing your infographic resume to someone you are meeting with instead of your wordy resume or bio.

Proof

Given the choice, would you rather read this?

Infographic production increases 1% every year.
90% of information that comes to the brain is visual.
13 million results for the term *infographic* on Google.
They catch the eye of journalists and stand out from dull text-based press releases.
Infographics help to visualize relationships and statistics simply and easily.
They show an expert understanding of a subject area or topic.
40% of people will respond better to visual information than text.
22% of infographics assessed use pie charts.
24% of infographics assessed use line charts.
32% of infographics assessed use bar graphs.
24% of infographics assessed use pictorial charts.

Or Figure 5-1?

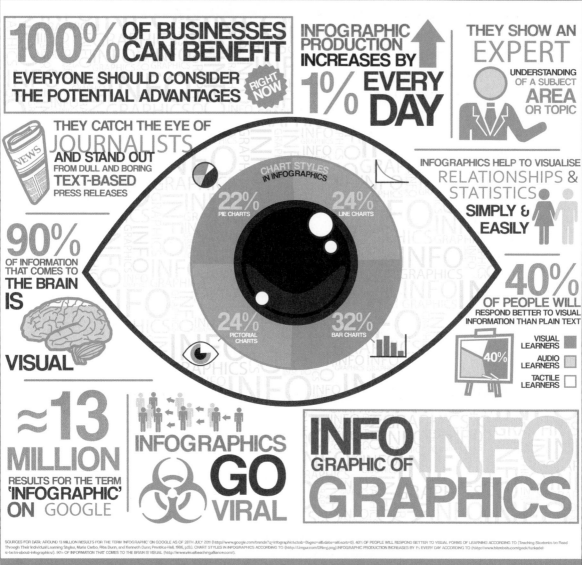

WATCH THIS SPACE. 'IN'
INFOGRAPHICS ARE IN

100% OF BUSINESSES CAN BENEFIT

EVERYONE SHOULD CONSIDER THE POTENTIAL ADVANTAGES

RIGHT NOW

INFOGRAPHIC PRODUCTION INCREASES BY **1%** EVERY DAY

THEY SHOW AN EXPERT UNDERSTANDING OF A SUBJECT AREA OR TOPIC

THEY CATCH THE EYE OF JOURNALISTS AND STAND OUT FROM DULL AND BORING TEXT-BASED PRESS RELEASES

NEWS

CHART STYLES IN INFOGRAPHICS

22% PIE CHARTS

24% LINE CHARTS

24% PICTORIAL CHARTS

32% BAR CHARTS

INFOGRAPHICS HELP TO VISUALISE RELATIONSHIPS & STATISTICS SIMPLY & EASILY

90% OF INFORMATION THAT COMES TO THE BRAIN IS VISUAL

40% OF PEOPLE WILL RESPOND BETTER TO VISUAL INFORMATION THAN PLAIN TEXT

VISUAL LEARNERS
AUDIO LEARNERS
TACTILE LEARNERS
40%

≈13 MILLION RESULTS FOR THE TERM 'INFOGRAPHIC' ON GOOGLE

INFOGRAPHICS GO VIRAL

INFO GRAPHIC OF INFO GRAPHICS

SOURCES FOR DATA: AROUND 13 MILLION RESULTS FOR THE TERM 'INFOGRAPHIC' ON GOOGLE AS OF 28TH JULY 2011 (http://www.google.com/trends?q=infographic&ctab=0&geo=all&date=all&sort=0). 40% OF PEOPLE WILL RESPOND BETTER TO VISUAL FORMS OF LEARNING ACCORDING TO (Teaching Students to Read Through Their Individual Learning Styles, Marie Carbo, Rita Dunn, and Kenneth Dunn; Prentice-Hall, 1986, p.13.). CHART STYLES IN INFOGRAPHICS ACCORDING TO (http://i.imgur.com/DNnrj.png).INFOGRAPHIC PRODUCTION INCREASES BY 1% EVERY DAY ACCORDING TO (http://www.bitrebels.com/geek/funkadel ic-facts-about-infographics/). 90% OF INFORMATION THAT COMES TO THE BRAIN IS VISUAL (http://www.visualteachingalliance.com/).

WWW.ENTROPII.COM

INFOGRAPHIC BROUGHT TO YOU BY **entropii**

FIGURE 5-1 **Infographic**

Who Is Using
Infographic Resumes?

You will see infographic resumes used by a wide variety of occupations. Technically anyone can use one; however, there are certain occupations and industries that are more likely to favor them, such as sales or marketing positions, design jobs, or any type of creative role. Industries that typically welcome out-of-the-ordinary resumes, based on success stories featured in this book, include marketing, advertising, communications, public relations, and new technology start-ups.

> A visual or infographic resume is likely to appeal to the reader, at least half the time, because approximately 65 percent of the population are visual learners, which means they prefer and retain images better than words.[5]

Infographics Used by Noncreatives

"I am not a graphic artist. I am not a marketer. I work in the field of disaster recovery and business continuity. My business card says 'counter terrorism and emergency management professional,' literally. One might suspect that folks in my profession don't take to visual marketing or visual resumes."

Kevin Burton's story began when he published his first visual resume in early 2010 as an exercise in visual communication. Kevin says, "At the time, there were very few visual resumes available online, so I had little to reference. The material that was out there was graphically intense and clearly crafted by graphic artists and the like. As an advisor to large organizations such as Cisco, Toyota, and Caterpillar, I had already taken note of the desire to express more in a single slide being voiced by several of my executive clients and thought a visual resume could be important for my future."

Kevin guessed correctly. "By 2013, the importance of my visual resume leaped out at me with utter clarity. While pitching a large city on my Disaster Recovery and Business Continuity Advisory services, I noticed that the clients were not reading my credentials from the proposal. Instead, someone had distributed a printed version of my original visual resume and the executives around the table were scanning it! The pages of credentials I had put into the proposal were useless to these accountants and lawyers. What mattered was my ability to summarize sixteen years of experience into a single visual."

Why This Works

Kevin Burton's infographic resume demonstrates his expertise and vast experience in the disaster recovery and emergency management world. He breaks from the vertical layout and uses the horizontal format to set his infographic apart from the masses. Kevin uses three easy-to-remember points at the top with a clear call to action. Recognizable corporate logos, a word cloud of prominent skills, and evidence of expertise follow the three-important-things-to-remember theme. The massive work history graph on the bottom reinforces his experience in his area of expertise. (See Figure 5-2.)

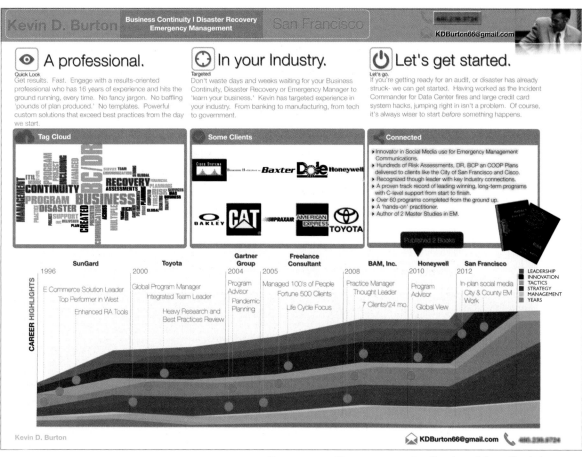

FIGURE 5-2 **Emergency Management Professional** http://bit.ly/1pt0BHo

Why This Works

Sneha Kochak includes a work timeline to show his professional and educational history, which conveys his commitment to learning and staying current on new trends in his field. He also uses a word-cloud element to show his technical skills. The larger the word, the stronger the skill. A pictograph shows hours he spends in outside interests, many of which align with his field of work and would presumably give him a greater appreciation for the needs of users in his user design profession. Sneha's infographic resume serves as a summary for the text version of his resume, which follows. By including the two versions, he addresses the preferences of both the visual and the traditional resume reviewer audiences. (See Figure 5-3.)

Sneha Kochak

Career timeline & resume

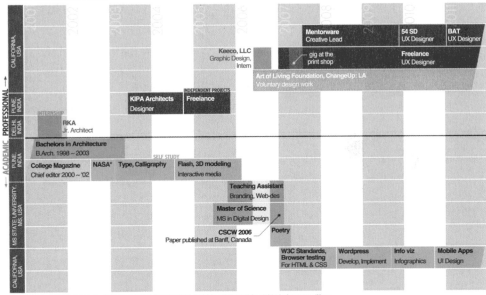

Professional:

Mentorware Creative Lead	**54 SD** UX Designer	**BAT** UX Designer
Keeco, LLC Graphic Design, Intern	gig at the print shop	**Freelance** UX Designer
Art of Living Foundation, ChangeUp: LA Voluntary design work		

KIPA Architects Designer

INDEPENDENT PROJECTS **Freelance**

INTERNSHIP

RKA Jr. Architect

Academic:

Bachelors in Architecture B.Arch. 1998 ~ 2003

College Magazine Chief editor 2000 ~ '02

NASA* **Type, Calligraphy**

SELF STUDY

Flash, 3D modeling Interactive media

Teaching Assistant Branding, Web-des

Master of Science MS in Digital Design

CSCW 2006 Paper published at Banff, Canada

Poetry

W3C Standards, Browser testing For HTML & CSS	**Wordpress** Develop, Implement	**Info viz** Infographics	**Mobile Apps** UI Design

***NASA:** National Association of Students of Architecture, India - multiple architectural & graphic design competitions

---

Beyond the nine to five:
in alphabetical order

blogging
research and/or expressions on twitter, tumblr & wordpress

creative writing
research and/or expressions on twitter, tumblr & wordpress

music
ambient/electronic/pop or playing the keyboard/guitar

racquetball
a couple of games a week at the university gym

swimming
5-10 laps a day, 3-4 times a week

yoga
basic yoga to stay toned & stay refreshed

01 02 03 04 05 06 07 08 09 10
← time spent in hours per week →

Skills:
in order of strengths, descending

UX design
Visual/Graphic design
Branding
Websites
UI design
Flash
Video
Storyboarding
Wordpress
Information visualization
3D-modeling
Web development

FIGURE 5-3 **Technical Designer** http://bitly.com/Kh75rR

SNEHA KOCHAK e: snehakochak@gmail.com
w: www.svish.com, www.snehakochak.com

Master of Science (MS)
College of Architecture, Art + Design (CAAD)
Mississippi State University (MSU)
Emphasis in Digital Design
December 2006

Professional Skills
UX Design, UI Design, Visual Design
Information Architecture, Information visualization
Brand identity, Graphic design
HTML & CSS, Storytelling & Video editing

Experience

March '11 to present
UX Designer
Brand Affinity Technologies
Irvine, California

September '09 to present
Freelance UX Designer (LA Area)
HP, Sony PlayStation, Xperience Interactive,
Falkon Productions, The Monsoon Company
Irvine, California

August '07 to August '09
Creative Lead
Mentorware Inc
Santa Clara, California

Jan '07 to August '09
Freelance Visual/UI Designer (SFBA)
California

Jun '06 to Aug '06
Graphic Designer
Keeco, LLC – Graphics
South San Francisco

Aug '05 to Dec '06
Research + Teaching Assistant
Design Research & Informatics Lab (DRIL)
Mississippi State University

May '06 to present
Graphic Designer
The Art of Living Foundation (non-profit
organization)
San Francisco Bay Area, USA

May '03 – Jul '05
Presentation & Graphic design
KIPA Architects
Pune, India

Tools (Advanced skills)

Adobe Photoshop CS5
Adobe Illustrator CS5
Adobe Flash CS5
Adobe Fireworks CS5
Adobe Dreamweaver CS5
Adobe Indesign CS5

OmniGraffle
Axure RP Pro
Adobe Premiere Pro, After Effects
3D Studio Max, Rhinoceros, Sketchup
Microsoft Visio
Microsoft Office Suite

Web Design
Advanced skills in front-end website/UI design as well as visual design. Proficient with HTML 5, XHTML, CSS 3, Flash action script 3.0; Experience with JavaScript, AJAX and Adobe Flex.

FIGURE 5-3 **Technical Designer** *(continued)*

SNEHA KOCHAK
Skills

Experience details

Brand Affinity Technologies (current): Worked on various marketing campaigns for celebrities, user interfaces for in-house content management software, mobile applications, Fantapper website as well as redesign, and graphics for multiple celebrities' branding.

Freelance (LA area): Worked with companies like HP, Xperience Interactive, 54 System Design, THQ, Sony Playstation, Falkon Productions, The Monsoon Company and BT Imaging - Experience in websites for video games and gaming console UI, video game publisher websites, SEO and CMS integration. Worked with start-ups on online applications and mobile applications. Created brand image and UI guidelines. Extensive work on software customizations for clients and creating homogenous visuals for all the company's products.

Creative Lead (Mentorware, Inc): Worked on Visual & UI development projects with companies such as Sun, Lenovo, Hitachi, Credence, and TIBCO. Job functions included UI design, visual design, web design and branding – developing 2D and well as 3D graphical interfaces for various rich-media information portals, community portals, desktop and web applications.

Freelance (SFBA): Worked with OnStor Storage Solutions (LSI Corporation), Virident Systems, bHive Software, Lenovo Training Solutions, Hitachi Data Systems. Undertook projects with various start-ups and worked on websites, user interfaces, product branding, print production and 3D immersive environments.

Assistantship: Digital design process study, surveys for research projects and marketing material development for the Design Research & Informatics Lab (DRIL) at CAAD, Mississippi State University. **Teaching** sessions on various graphic design software and strategies, Digital Design processes and integrating software with traditional media.

Achievements and Publications
- Awarded a **full scholarship** by Mississippi State University at the MS in Architecture program at the CAAD.
- Poster 'Design of a Personal Interface in a University Gymnasium to Encourage Student Usage' **published** at CSCW 2006, Banff, Canada.
- Ongoing **research** in 'Information design for the blind'.

Tools
- **Visual Design:**
  Adobe Photoshop CS5, Adobe Illustrator CS5, Adobe Dreamweaver CS5, Adobe Acrobat, Alias Sketchbook Pro, Google Sketchup, 3D Studio Max
- **Prototyping & Wireframing**:
  OmniGraffle, Axure RP Pro, Microsoft Visio, Adobe Fireworks, Alias Sketchbook Pro (+ Wacom Tablet), Pencil & Paper (!)
- **Multimedia:**
  Adobe Flash, Adobe Premiere Pro, Adobe After Effects.
- **Scripting:**
  HTML, XHTML, CSS, Flash Action scripting.
- **Office Management:**
  Microsoft Office 2007 Suite, Microsoft Groove, Microsoft Project, Aperture, Adobe Lightroom, Comfortable with both, Mac as well as Windows based environments

Extra Activities:
- **Creative writing,** especially poetry. I've taken extra credits at graduate school in the English department in **poetry**. I've been the magazine editor at high school and college.
- Playing the Hawaiian **guitar**. I've undergone training in classical Indian music for 8 years and have a senior diploma from Prayag University, Allahabad, India.
- **Racquetball** (and/or swimming) on a daily basis and **Meditating**.

FIGURE 5-3 **Technical Designer** *(continued)*

81

Why This Works

Colleen Havens's infographic resume begins with a welcoming message to the reader. This infographic uses different types of bar charts, pie charts, and doughnuts, as well as a Venn diagram, to summarize her skills and areas of knowledge. Color is another element that ties this resume together. A scannable QR code at the bottom links to her portfolio. And for those familiar with pop culture, she's included a reference to a popular song that also serves as a call to action to contact her. (See Figure 5-4.)

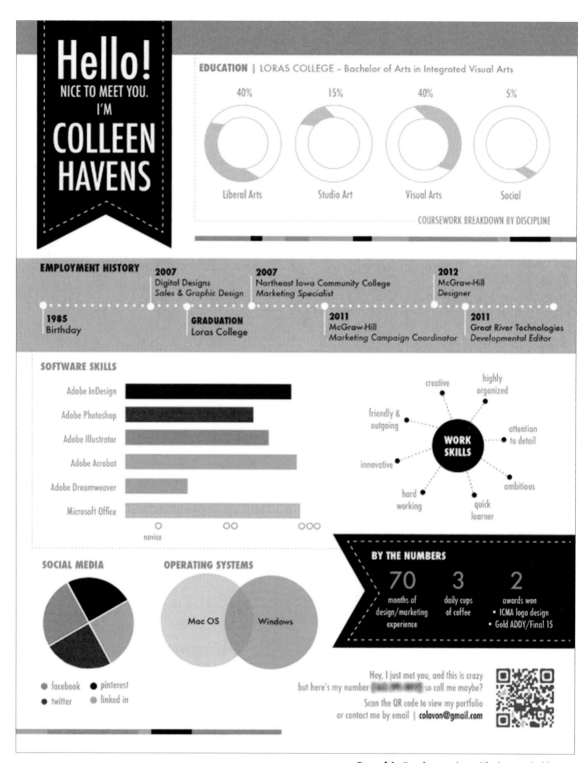

FIGURE 5-4 **Graphic Designer** http://bitly.com/1dtbBQV

Why This Works

Daniel Tewfik uses color, logos, and photos to keep this infographic resume uncluttered and high impact. He shows his broad range of industry expertise with recognizable company logos that correspond to a color-coded timeline. Daniel conveys his unique blend of creative and analytical knowledge by highlighting his design skills. Blue banners mark the sections of his work experience, education, skills, and interests to clearly delineate call-out features. Placed strategically at the bottom are photographs showing Daniel's favorite activities. By sharing his personal interests, Daniel's resume becomes more personal and potentially connects him to the reader. (See Figure 5-5.)

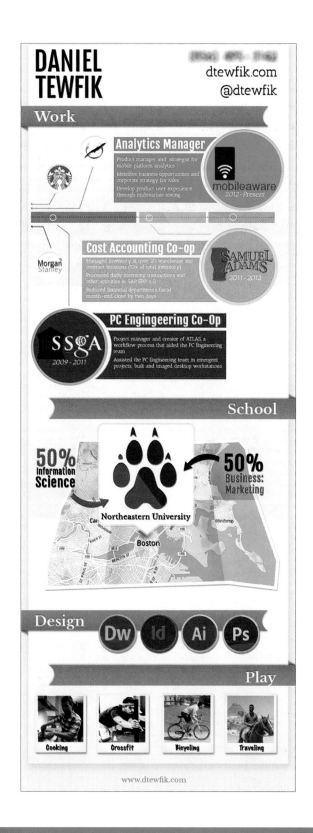

85

Why This Works

Anjana Jayaweera uses icons, graphs, charts, and a work timeline blended together on this infographic. What makes this a standout infographic is the section entitled "why we should work together?" in which he calls out the qualities that will make him a valuable employee and a good fit for the organization's culture. The personal information on the bottom of this resume may not be necessary or relevant, depending on the country you are from. Multiple contact options also makes it easy connect. (See Figure 5-6.)

FIGURE 5-6 **Designer** http://bitly.com/1kAdpvy

Why This Works

Sheng Fen Chien's infographic uses subtle coordinated colors, icons, doughnut charts depicting skill levels, and a timeline with icons, all tied together for this communications specialist. The banner at the top states her attributes and focus, and to round out her story, she includes her personal interests at the bottom, many of which correspond nicely with her career focus. (See Figure 5-7.)

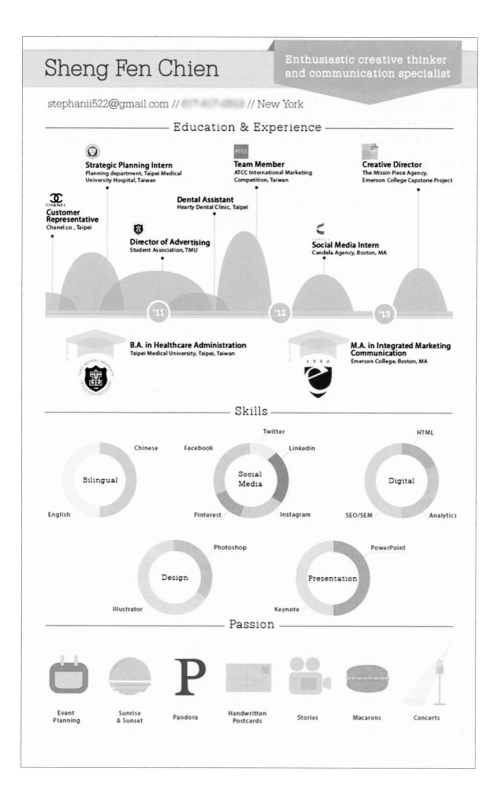

Why This Works

Brad Crabtree clearly establishes his focus and expertise—social media strategist, community manager, and online communication. He backs up his claim by including his social media accounts. Brad summarizes his career and lists industry experience to hone his message at the very top of his infographic. He has listed testimonials on the right side to offer social proof. Numbers speak, so Brad has listed some key stats to show his key accomplishments, skills, and expertise. (See Figure 5-8.)

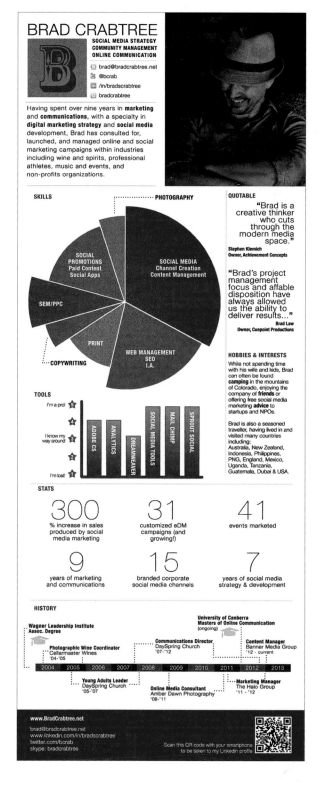

Why This Works

John Miller has used a variety of infographic elements and pictures to show areas of knowledge, starting with his scope of work. Maps, timeline, line graph, and three-dimensional chart provide alternative methods for John to share his message. (See Figure 5-9.)

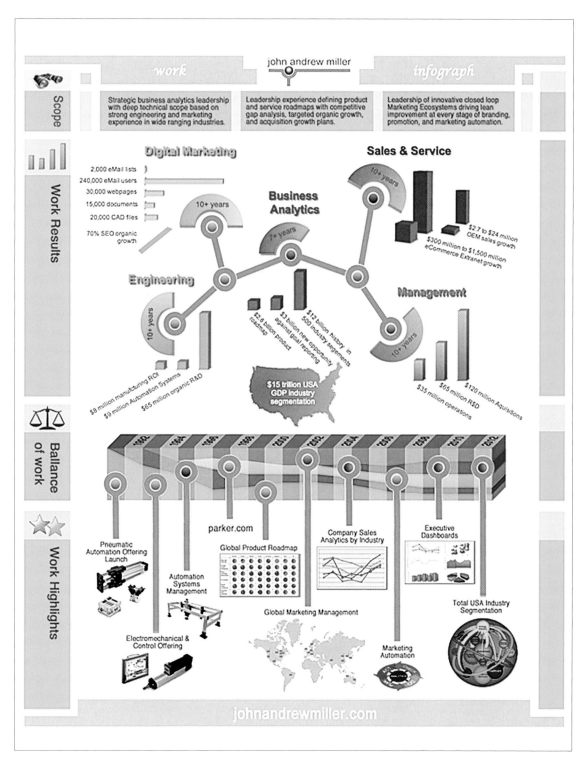

FIGURE 5-9 **Digital Marketing** http://bit.ly/1dtc6KS

Why This Works

Mike-Anthony Saade concocts just the right magic with his use of color and nod to wizardry. His story begins with words from a Pokémon theme song, and he continues to use the magic theme throughout the document, listing weapons and professional attributes. Saade's outside interests help the reader understand his fascination with anime, video games, and some out-of-the-ordinary surprises. (See Figure 5-10.)

MIKE-ANTHONY SAADE
GRAPHIC DESIGN WIZARD // LEVEL 21

STORY OBJECTIVE:
I WANNA BE THE VERY BEST,
LIKE NO ONE EVER WAS!

EXPERIENCE GAINED

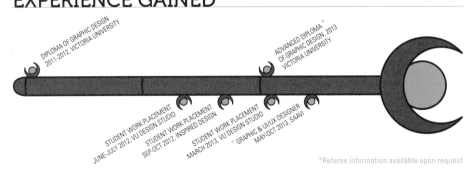

DIPLOMA OF GRAPHIC DESIGN
2011-2012, VICTORIA UNIVERSITY

ADVANCED DIPLOMA
OF GRAPHIC DESIGN, 2013
VICTORIA UNIVERSITY

STUDENT WORK PLACEMENT
JUNE-JULY 2012, VU DESIGN STUDIO

STUDENT WORK PLACEMENT
SEP-OCT 2012, INSPIRED DESIGN

STUDENT WORK PLACEMENT
MARCH 2013, VU DESIGN STUDIO

GRAPHIC & UI/UX DESIGNER
MAY-OCT 2013, SAAVI

*Referee information available upon request

SPECIALTY MAGIC

BRANDING   PRINT DESIGN   UI/UX DESIGN   ILLUSTRATION

WEAPONS

 Id
 Ai
 Ps

 Fl
 W
 Dw

SIDEQUESTS

 FASHION
 FOOD
 DRINKS

 TV
 MOVIES
 MUSIC

 アニメ ANIME
 POCKET MONSTERS
 VIDEO GAMES

 WINTER
 CONFETTI
PSYCHIC POWERS

ATTRIBUTES

VIBRANCY   PERFECTIONISM   RELIABILITY   ORGANISATION   CREATIVITY

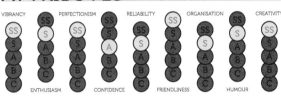

ENTHUSIASM   CONFIDENCE   FRIENDLINESS   HUMOUR

CONTACT

📞 ....
@ .... mike-anthony-@live.com
★ .... mikeanthonydesign.com
🐦 .... twitter.com/MikeAnthonyGD
⚃ .... theloop.com.au/mike-anthony
Be .... behance.net/mike-anthony

FIGURE 5-10 **Graphic Design Wizard** http://bit.ly/1lDHQgQ

Why This Works

Shirley Schutt is a web designer, and her message is simple and straightforward. She loves what she does and includes a Venn diagram to show how her areas of knowledge intersect. Shirley uses a branding statement to spell out her value to employers, and she clearly supplies a call to action—Hire me! Unified colors and stacked bar graphs and icons help complete the uncomplicated infographic. (See Figure 5-11.)

SHIRLEY SCHUTT

Web and Graphic Designer

HIRE ME

PRINT · BRANDING · MARKETING · WEB

I LOVE WHAT I DO ♥

I LIKE TO CREATIVELY PROBLEM SOLVE AND UNCOVER NEEDS!

CONTACT

 Yonkers, NY 10701

 (XXX) XXX-XXXX

✉ hello@shirleyschutt.com

🐦 @OhShirl

🌐 www.shirleyschutt.com
www.ohshirl.com

INTERESTS

TIMELINE

EDUCATION | EXPERIENCE

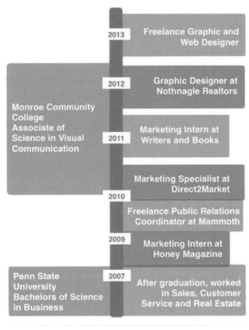

2013 — Freelance Graphic and Web Designer

2012 — Graphic Designer at Nothnagle Realtors

Monroe Community College
Associate of Science in Visual Communication

2011 — Marketing Intern at Writers and Books

2010 — Marketing Specialist at Direct2Market

Freelance Public Relations Coordinator at Mammoth

2009 — Marketing Intern at Honey Magazine

Penn State University
Bachelors of Science in Business

2007 — After graduation, worked in Sales, Customer Service and Real Estate

SKILLS

- ADOBE ILLUSTRATOR
- HTML
- CSS
- ADOBE INDESIGN
- JQUERY
- WORDPRESS
- MARKETING
- ADOBE PHOTOSHOP
- JAVASCRIPT
- PHP

FIGURE 5-11
Web and Graphic Designer
http://bit.ly/19skBF4

97

Why This Works

Hagan Blount, a designer, has included a wealth of information about his expertise in his infographic resume. His mission statement at the top provides insight into his personality, purpose, and guiding force. He includes testimonials from raving fans, and his stats section shows numbers designed to impress. We'll hear more from Hagan in Chapter 6, where he talks about designing infographic resumes for clients. (See Figure 5-12.)

HAGAN BLOUNT
+CURRICULUM VITAE

Notes:

MISSION STATEMENT: *I am a radiating center of universal love. By producing things that assist, entertain, and inspire others, my light spreads over the world.*

BRIEF HISTORY:

1. I was born in Portland, ME. I grew up around New England and New York
2. I went to college at Rensselaer Polytechnic Institute in New York
3. Post-Graduation, I spent six months in China teaching English and traveling
4. After China, I took a job in DC and explored the beltway for five years
5. In 2006, I got a few friends together to try and buy a volcano in the Aleutian islands
6. I moved to Boston in 2007 for a girl
7. When we broke up, I bought a motorcycle in Costa Rica and saw all of Central America
8. I bought an RV and started filming a pilot for the Food Network. Ran out of money
9. So I "sold" my condo in Baltimore, moved to New York City, and made this infographic résumé
10. I started designing them for others, so I saw Peru, Ecuador, Colombia, Cuba, and Mexico for six months, making résumés & traveling
11. Now I'm back in NYC looking for life's next big challenge in spending 110% of my motivation kicking ass for you and your brands!

CAREER:

 NANHAI NORMAL SCHOOL : TEACHER
I made a evaluation sheet for my students to fill about me around mid-semester. One of them said I was "killing her spirit for learning." Fixed that. I mean come on - it was my first time teaching. Learned that my way of life is not always the right way.

 GE GXS : FINANCIAL MANAGEMENT PROGRAM
Big finance. Learned that I didn't want to be an accountant for the rest of my life.
INSIDE SALES
Learned that everyone is marketing themselves or just waiting to die.

 PRIMERICA FINANCIAL SERVICES : SALES
Financial planner. A few MM of assets under management, marketed insurance and mortgages. Learned I was a better salesperson than recruiter.

 CALUSA INVESTMENTS : BROKER
Made more money in three months than I had any year prior. Plenty of sales awards. didn't think subprime loans were all that awful. They called me, so I felt I was giving them what they *wanted*. Learned not to tell people what I thought they *needed*.

 INTERFICIO ASSASSINATION TOURNAMENT
Ran watergun assassination tournaments in Chicago, D.C.,& Austin. Worked with my brother and multiple programmers developing a text-based "kill confirmation" system. Learned that to have success, you need to share the vision.

 AMERICAN TOWER : TOWER ACQUISITIONS
Assigned a budget to buy out cell tower leases. Taught new reps sales skills in team call nights, instructed reps on new CRM system. In the end, didn't think deals were all that great. Learned that you have to believe in what you're selling to sell.

 WANDERING FOODIE : WRITER
Decided I was going to take my money from mortgages and film a pilot for the Food Network. Shot at 24 restaurants in 24 Hours in DC, Boston. Ran out of money, moved to NYC. Learned that it's easy to enter a scene if you make friends with bloggers.

 MORRIS + KING : SOCIAL MEDIA CONSULTANT
Strategy for Classic Media, Digital Broadcasting Group, Social Media Week. Learned that if your client thinks something is funny, it's best just to laugh along with them.

 INGK LABS : ENTREPRENEUR IN RESIEDNCE
Brought Ingk the concept for a next generation customer service platform utilizing semi-automatic responses driven by natural language processing. Learned that managing projects from South American Hostels is doable.

TECHNICAL SKILL DEVELOPMENT

1998 1999 2000 2001 2002 2003 2004 2005 2006 2007 2008 2009 2010 2011 2012

PRESS HITS
WEB ADS
TWITTER
VIDEO PRODUCTION
EXCEL
CSS
HTML
COMING UP WITH AWESOME IDEAS
WRITING
SALES

COLLEGE:

 RENSSELAER POLYTECHNIC INSTITUTE
B.S. in Management Concentrations in Finance and IT Management

PROJECTS:

 LIKESTICKERS.NET
Like things in real life with "Like Stickers." The #1 result on Google for like stickers. Facebook knows about them. They're cool with it.

I TASTE YOUR BEER
In 2011, I made a living drinking beer (and making promotional videos for microbreweries). Tough job, but someone's gotta do it.

PRAISE:

"Hagan's services are awesome, especially if your brand is active in the social media realm."
Jim Crooks
VP Marketing
Narragansett Beer

"He's committed to getting results quickly."
Hazel Courteney
Columnist
The Daily Mail

"You can train a lion. You don't teach a lamb to be a lion. Hagan is a lion."
Dave Shumway
CEO
Calusa Investments

STATS:

60,000
Words I wrote in January 2010

242
≈700 word posts written in 2010

176
Press hits from 2010 to 2012

10 Million
Approximate number of people who have seen my résumés

112,000
Traffic as a result of this CV, May 2011

37
Purported number of Justin Biebers I can take in a fight

16,000
Number of real Twitter followers amassed for myself & others

1...
...more guy you need on your team to make a big impact on the bottom line

REACH ME ANYTIME:

 • IAm@HaganBlount.com
http://HaganBlount.com • Twitter.com/Hagan

FIGURE 5-12 **Designer** http://bit.ly/1dNz0Yo

99

INFOGRAPHIC RESUMES

Why This Works

Paolo Zupin uses white space to divide his document. Through his use of a variety of visual elements, from bar graphs to world maps and timelines, we can see the span of his experience. Paolo includes a QR code that can be scanned to upload his contact information into a recruiter's smartphone. In European-style resumes, it is common to see date of birth; however, in most U.S. resumes, this is not advisable. (See Figure 5-13.)

PAOLO ZUPIN
RESUME

DATE OF BIRTH: *21/08/1984*
ADDRESS: *via Amendola 1/2*
34134 Trieste, Italy
MOBILE:
E-MAIL: *paolo.zupin@gmail.com*
WEBSITE: *www.paolozupin.com*

WORK EXPERIENCE ▾

● **WEB MARKETING SPECIALIST**

@ SCHIBELLO CAFFÈ: *Schibello caffè is a coffee company with a **strong Italian Heritage**, based in **Sydney** and with branch offices in Brisbane and Melbourne.*

- *Developed and managed company's website*
- *Analyzed marketing campaign performance.*
- *Designed and managed short and long-term online content strategies.*
- *Reviewed and monitored the internet for branding opportunities and company's web presence.*
- *Established and applied the guidelines for social media presence.*

12/2010 - 08/2011   ⦿ SYDNEY, AUS

● **JUNIOR SALE PROFESSIONAL**

@ ALLEANZA ASSICURAZIONI: *Alleanza Assicurazioni S.p.A. operates in the life insurance industry in Italy and other parts of Europe.*

- *Customized insurance programs to suit individual customers, often covering a variety of risks.*
- *Sought out new clients and develop clientele by networking to find new customers and generate lists of prospective clients.*

09/2010 - 12/2010   ⦿ TRIESTE, IT

EDUCATION ▾

IULM	UNIVERSITY OF TRIESTE	UNIVERSITY OF TRIESTE
SOCIAL MEDIA MARKETING E WEB COMMUNICATION EXECUTIVE MASTER	**INTERNATIONAL ECONOMICS AND CURRENCY MARKETS** MASTER OF SCIENCE	**INTERNATIONAL ECONOMICS AND CURRENCY MARKETS** BACHELOR'S OF SCIENCE
	• *Degree Thesis: "Social Networks and Organization"*	• *Degree Thesis: "Ebay, Business Model and Organization"*
	• *Final Mark: 106/110*	• *Final Mark: 102/110*
01-12/2012 ⦿ MILANO, IT	2006/2008 ⦿ TRIESTE, IT	2003/2006 ⦿ TRIESTE, IT

*TOEFL TEST 09/2009 (score: 101/120, internet based) ⦿ *San Diego, CA*

TIME LINE ▾

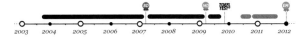

2003   2004   2005   2006   2007   2008   2009   2010   2011   2012

STATS ▾

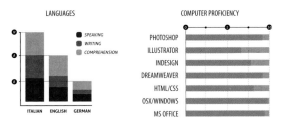

LANGUAGES

- SPEAKING
- WRITING
- COMPREHENSION

ITALIAN   ENGLISH   GERMAN

COMPUTER PROFICIENCY

PHOTOSHOP
ILLUSTRATOR
INDESIGN
DREAMWEAVER
HTML/CSS
OSX/WINDOWS
MS OFFICE

WHO AM I ? ▾

BROADMINDED · CONSISTENT · COHERENT · ANALYTICAL · EFFICIENT · ORGANIZED · RELIABLE · HONEST · HARDWORKING · AMBITIOUS

PAOLO

INTERNATIONAL EXPERIENCE ▾

SAN DIEGO   TRIESTE   SYDNEY

INTERESTS ▾

WEB 2.0   **WEB-MARKETING**
INFORMATION TECHNOLOGY
S.E.O. SOCIAL MEDIA
MOBILE APPS *SPORT* MUSIC
HTML/CSS SOCIAL NETWORKS
WEB DESIGN VIDEO-EDITING
SOCCER *READING* **MOBILE**
COMPUTING **UI-DESIGN**
YOU TUBE

QRCODE BUSINESS CARD ▾

* Scan the code to get my contact details!

FIGURE 5-13 **Web Marketing Professional** http://bit.ly/1d0UyDa

101

Why This Works

Greg Gonzalez's infographic resume simply outlines his thought process and the focus of his design work. He uses images and words to define his work and a colorful curved timeline to show his education. In order to demonstrate his skill level, he uses pyramid-shaped bar charts and software icons. Greg's work experience is conveyed through a timeline as well as text to ensure his career story is understood. (See Figure 5-14.)

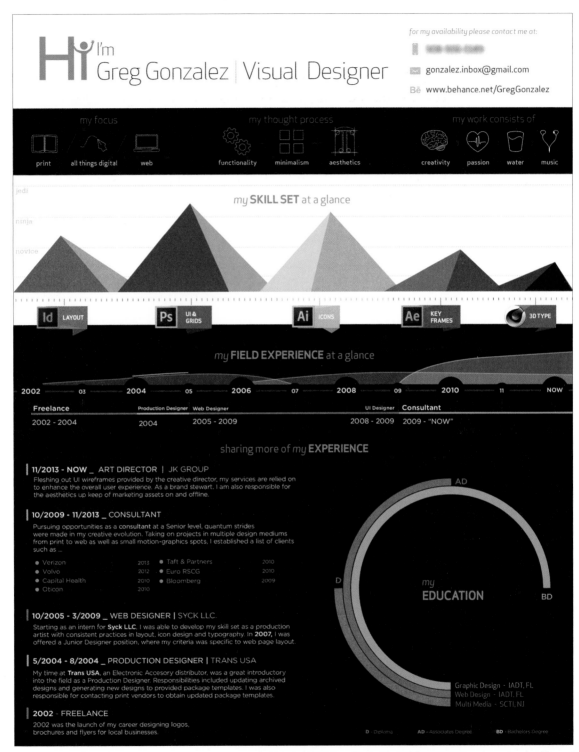

Why This Works

Steve Williams is a designer and trainer, adept at meeting the unique visual needs of learners. His resume uses all the expected infographic elements and is laid out to look like uncluttered presentation slides. The head-and-upper-torso shots in his resume convey his comfort in front of the camera and probably in front of the room too. (See Figures 5-15a and b.)

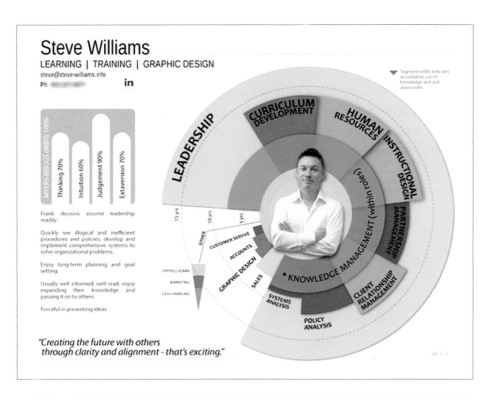

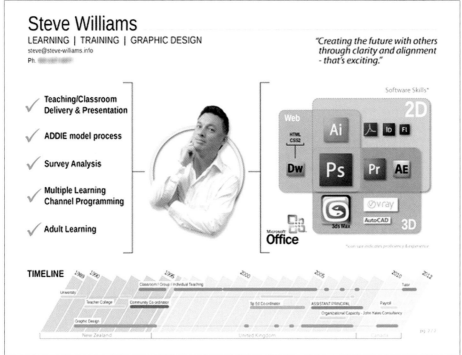

FIGURES 5-15a and b
**Learning and
Development and
Graphic Design**
http://bit.ly/L0xXgz

105

Why This Works

Michelle Campbell's strong illustration and design skills are clearly evident in her resume. She creatively uses a tree to show professional growth and includes key stats to help pack a meaningful punch. Michelle's contemporary color scheme and design elements all come together. (See Figure 5-16.)

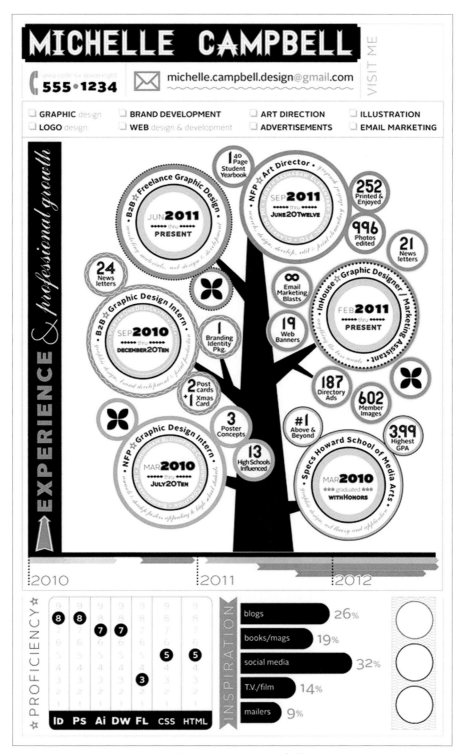

FIGURE 5-16 **Graphic Design, Brand Development, and Illustration** http://bit.ly/1gFPzJ3

Eliza Doton's resume has a very specific audience. Her resume is emulating the feel of a Pinterest page. It highlights work history with a combination of pictures and words and also features some of her key achievements. It's creative, and it demonstrates her interest in social media and important skill sets. (See Figure 5-17.)

The Beauty Is in Shareability

Infographics are trendy. In two years, search traffic volume for infographics increased 800 percent, according to Google Trends.[6] Marketers realize that a post or update with an infographic will generate more traffic, and you can leverage this marketing power too. Imagine how great it would be to publish your infographic online and find that people like it so much they share it with their networks. This doesn't always happen, but it is always a possibility.

Once you create your infographic, give it a home. You may decide it will reside on your website, and this is the best place for it. Another option is to host it on Visual.ly. But don't count on the fact that people will find it and automatically share it. You will have to draw attention to your infographic by circulating a link to it among your network. Upload your infographic to your LinkedIn profile summary as embedded media and share a link to your infographic resume as a status update on LinkedIn too. But don't stop there. Share it as a status update on all your social networks; even include it as a link on your e-mail signature. You can learn more about how to share and draw attention to your infographic resume in Chapter 11.

Success Stories

There are numerous success stories of job seekers who've stepped outside the box to garner the attention of hiring managers. In the previous chapter, you saw the Amazonlike resume of Philippe Dubost.

FIGURE 5-17

Marketing Professional and Avid Pinterest Fan

http://bit.ly/1do3Muh

109

Chris Spurlock is another success story. His resume includes a clever timeline of his experiences, as well as a graph illustrating his skills. After sharing his infographic resume on HuffPost College, Chris's resume was shared all over the web and attracted interest from many employers. Once he graduated from college, Chris secured a job as an infographic design editor with the *Huffington Post*.

Generating Ideas Is Only Step One

As you review the samples in this chapter, there are certain resumes that probably resonate with you. Your preferences are part of your style. Use your gut as a guiding principle for the next phase. When you think about creating your own resume, which graphs did you like best and which will best illustrate your skills? Don't get sidetracked by the "doing" part or not knowing how you would create the chart; it may limit your creativity. There are tools and advice in Chapter 7 to help you create infographics. Also think about the sections or elements you want to include on your resume. Did you like seeing how the interests were conveyed with pictures, or are you more of an icon person? Or perhaps you hadn't even thought of including your interests before seeing these. Collecting ideas is the start for determining how you will present your qualifications in your infographic resume.

CHAPTER 6

Professionally Crafted Infographic Resumes

If you want a unique visual resume but don't have the design skills to create one, you should know that there are designers who specialize in creating infographic resumes. Think about the time it would take you to learn the software, understand how to best lay out your design, plus figure out which chart or graph to use. That can add up. It is common for people to outsource work to get the best possible results. If you aren't a plumber, you probably wouldn't tackle installing a brand-new sink or toilet. You save time, money, and sanity in the long run by hiring someone who specializes in that area of work.

You have at least a couple of different options to contract someone to do your infographic resume, and this chapter will show your where to find someone to design your infographic resume should you decide to go this route.

Get a Winning Design

Another outsourcing option is to use a site like 99designs.com and ask designers to submit a quote or bid for your infographic resume project. As a client on 99designs, you hold a contest. You describe what you are looking for, and designers submit a draft of their work for you to review. You can even ask people you know to review the submitted designs and vote for the ones they like best. The cost to enter as a client or contest holder starts at $249 to $999, depending on the number of designs you would like to see. Figure 6-1 shows the winning design selected from 99designs by product manager Jason Toff.

Here are some resources for finding a graphic designer to help with your infographic resume. All these sites similarly serve as marketplaces to connect employers hiring freelancers in software development, writing, data entry, design, engineering, the sciences, sales and marketing, accounting, and legal services.

- CrowdSpring (http://www.crowdspring.com)
- Freelancer (http://www.freelancer.com)

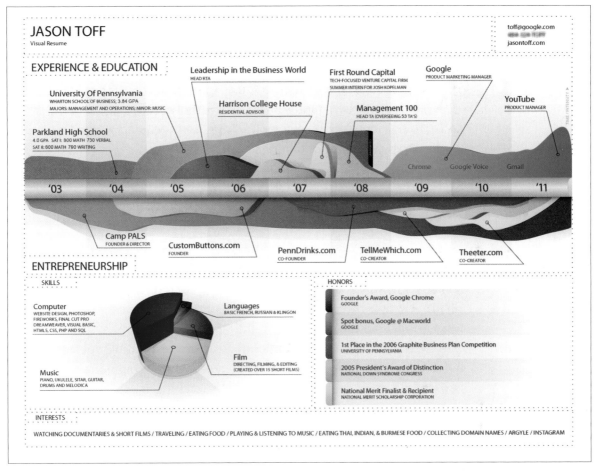

FIGURE 6-1
Example of Final Design Put Out to Bid
http://bit.ly/1jE2BqK

- Elance (http://www.elance.com)
- Guru (http://www.guru.com)
- ODesk (http://www.odesk.com)

You can also visit portfolio sites like the ones listed below to search the portfolios and work done by designers. If you decide to contact a designer through one of these sites, you will work with that person directly throughout the process. Pricing will depend on the individual designer.

- Behance (http://www.behance.net). Creative work showcased through this online platform hosting a growing collection of over 50 million images

113

- **Carbonmade** (https://carbonmade.com/). An online portfolio featuring more than 1.6 million projects by creatives and artists
- **DeviantArt** (http://www.deviantart.com). A network of 28 million registered members representing all forms of creative art
- **Dribbble** (http://dribbble.com/). Design portfolios and work samples from thousands of different designers

Anyone Can Have an Infographic Resume

The resumes on the following pages represent a collection of professionals from diverse backgrounds. They were created by Hagan Blount. He calls himself a project manager, but what he does is closer to an art director and personal branding designer. Hagan says that in 2011 he was one of the first nondesigners to create an infographically based resume. The month after he created his infographic resume, two people—one of whom was actively seeking a job—commissioned him to do theirs. And in fact, the resume he did for the active job seeker resulted in his client landing a dream job.

Why This Works

The yellow background makes this resume stand out. Yellow communicates optimism and may even stimulate creative thought. In Chapter 7, you'll learn more about the significance of color. This resume includes a branding statement and, under each area of specialty, a short statement about the value Daniel brings to his next employer. An area graph shows how this candidate improved brand engagement. What you'll notice about this infographic resume is that the graphs show results and accomplishments that are the differentiators employers are looking for. (See Figure 6-2.)

Daniel Brienza

Bring your brands to life.

As the Global Director for a leading triathlon event business, founder of a media group and athlete management organization, and a National Director of Marketing for Toyota, Daniel Brienza brings you the business-boosting resources and tools you need to deliver innovative ideas with speed and efficiency. Through strategy, marketing, budgeting, and bootstrapping he can produce tremendous results, with even the most extreme constraints.

Brand Management
Unforgettable marketing comes from bold instincts and careful planning. With Daniel, you'll get brand management that is fearless, smart — and proven in its effectiveness again and again.

370% Grew Toyota's Sponsorship Recall in endurance sports vertical market from 24% to 89% in 3 years

3 product launches executed for Toyota resulting in sales of **$25MM+** in new vertical markets

$18MM+ In marketing programs managed such as Toyota in Triathlons, the NBA, Farmer's Markets, and Dog Shows. You heard me; Dog Shows sell cars

12% increase in click-through rates after redefining LT's CRM system

27% increase in sales recorded after redefinition of LTF's customer outreach system

150% increase in website traffic recorded after redefining LTF's marketing and customer outreach strategy

Business Strategy
With keen insight into both short and long term business strategy, Daniel can position your business for dynamic future growth. A flexible and smart strategist, Daniel has an impressive track record for strategic planning and team management.

120+ events launched for Life Time Fitness

5 regional teams led

40+ team members managed

12% increase in marginal revenues and a 17.4% decrease in consumer time in the purchase funnel; from awareness to purchase. How? He built a consumer behavior theory model and pricing communications model for LTF to understand what the customers wanted—and how to deliver it effectively

20+ corporate partners brought on through his LTF sponsorship strategies

Business Development
As a team player with an authentic entrepreneurial spirit, Daniel offers a diverse set of experiences helping businesses of all sizes become industry leaders. For example:

27% Grew Life Time Fitness's Triathlon Division by 27% in 8.5 months

26% cost reduction for the combined business entity after he developed a merger integration strategy for Sprint and Nextel resulting in a more sophisticated vendor network and better customer support for both sides

Grew a small soccer coaching organization from **10k** in revenue to **$165k+** in 2.5 years

$4MM+ acquisition strategy executed for LTF in 2012; acquiring, combining and training 4 separate new business entities and their staff

Budget Management
Daniel's state-of-the-art financial management skills are perfectly positioned to master budgets of all sizes. See past successes here:

$70MM budget for 45+ experimental marketing programs maintained for Toyota

0 number of times he has gone over budget

$2MM+ budget programmed for LTF's triathlons events division, exceeding revenue targets for the first time in 5 years

1.2% margin of error on estimates 3 years running in managing Toyota's $70MM+ marketing budget

Process Improvement
A fierce financial analyst with a background in both economics and client/vendor management, Daniel knows how businesses can and should work. With bold ideas and solid instincts, he'll help you trim down and speed up. His ideas have resulted in:

150+ employees optimized within a new customer support system & org structure resulting in 25% increase in customer retention as a Strategic Business Analyst for Accenture

10% cost reduction on LTF's outsourced services and products resulting from re-engineered purchase and RFP framework

35+ business operations standardized after he wrote the first-ever process roadmap for Saatchi & Saatchi

85+ processes and checklists re-engineered for Sprint-Nextel merger for Day 1

16% saved on all media campaigns by developing a new buying process media strategy for LTF

Optimize your business with Daniel's powerful collection of experience and skills

Phone: ███████ | **Email:** danieljbrienza@parkandpier.com | **Linkedin:** www.linkedin.com/in/danieljbrienza

EMPLOYMENT HISTORY

2009 – 2013
Founder, Park & Pier Media Group

2011 – 2012
Global Director, Life Time Fitness

2007 – 2011
National Marketing Director, Saatchi & Saatchi

2005 – 2006
Strategy Business Analyst, Accenture

2003 – 2007
Founder, Elite Sports Performance

2002
Professional Soccer Player, Sao Paolo FC

EDUCATION

Johns Hopkins University
MS, Applied Economics.

BS, Economics, Business Entrepreneurship & Mgmt. & Mathematical Sciences.

ADDED FEATURES

72 Triathlons completed with 16 first-place finishes

7 All-American awards in triathlon and soccer

4 countries lived in and languages spoken

2 kids have even more energy than he does

DANIEL DOES MORE WITH LESS
Daniel's Business Division

Budget Support 3.3%   **Total Sales** 26.35%

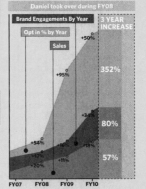

Daniel took over during FY08

Brand Engagements By Year | **3 YEAR INCREASE**

Opt in % by Year

+50%

Sales

+95%

352%

+34%

80%

+54%

+17%   +18%

+11%

57%

+20%

FY07   FY08   FY09   FY10

FIGURE 6-2 **Marketing and Business Strategy Professional**

Why This Works

Three simple phrases at the top define why this candidate is a must-hire. The style of this infographic is perhaps reminiscent of those seen in the mechanical engineering field. The summary gives an overview of the important experiences and challenges she has solved and is ready to solve for her next employer. Icons and images help the reader follow the sections and focus on keywords. A bar chart shows improvement in shipped product, just another example of an accomplishment an employer would be interested in. (See Figure 6-3.)

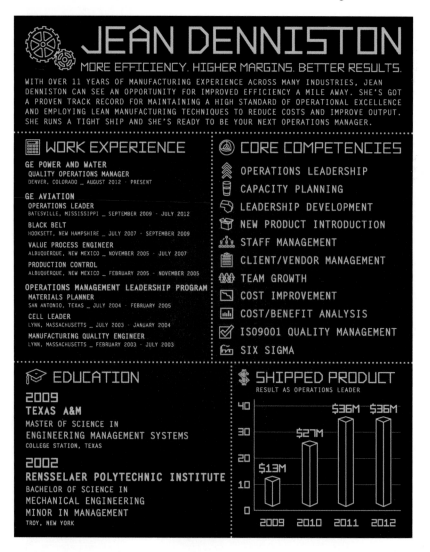

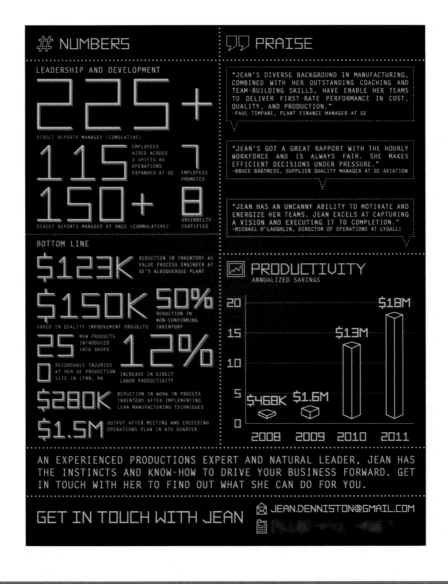

NUMBERS

LEADERSHIP AND DEVELOPMENT

225+
DIRECT REPORTS MANAGED (CUMULATIVE)

115
EMPLOYEES HIRED ACROSS 3 SHIFTS AS OPERATIONS EXPANDED AT GE

7
EMPLOYEES PROMOTED

150+
DIRECT REPORTS MANAGED AT ONCE (CUMMULATIVE)

8
GREENBELTS CERTIFIED

BOTTOM LINE

$123K
REDUCTION IN INVENTORY AS VALUE PROCESS ENGINEER AT GE'S ALBUQUERQUE PLANT

$150K
SAVED IN QUALITY IMPROVEMENT PROJECTS

50%
REDUCTION IN NON-CONFORMING INVENTORY

25
NEW PRODUCTS INTRODUCED INTO SHOPS

0
RECORDABLE INJURIES AT HER GE PRODUCTION SITE IN LYNN, MA

12%
INCREASE IN DIRECT LABOR PRODUCTIVITY

$280K
REDUCTION IN WORK IN PROCESS INVENTORY AFTER IMPLEMENTING LEAN MANUFACTURING TECHNIQUES

$1.5M
OUTPUT AFTER MEETING AND EXCEEDING OPERATIONS PLAN IN 4TH QUARTER

💬 PRAISE

"JEAN'S DIVERSE BACKGROUND IN MANUFACTURING, COMBINED WITH HER OUTSTANDING COACHING AND TEAM-BUILDING SKILLS, HAVE ENABLE HER TEAMS TO DELIVER FIRST-RATE PERFORMANCE IN COST, QUALITY, AND PRODUCTION."
-PAUL TIMPANE, PLANT FINANCE MANAGER AT GE

"JEAN'S GOT A GREAT RAPPORT WITH THE HOURLY WORKFORCE AND IS ALWAYS FAIR. SHE MAKES EFFICIENT DECISIONS UNDER PRESSURE."
-BRUCE BARTMESS, SUPPLIER QUALITY MANAGER AT GE AVIATION

"JEAN HAS AN UNCANNY ABILITY TO MOTIVATE AND ENERGIZE HER TEAMS. JEAN EXCELS AT CAPTURING A VISION AND EXECUTING IT TO COMPLETION."
-MICHAEL O'LAUGHLIN, DIRECTOR OF OPERATIONS AT LYDALLI

📈 PRODUCTIVITY
ANNUALIZED SAVINGS

	2008	2009	2010	2011
	$468K	$1.6M	$13M	$18M

AN EXPERIENCED PRODUCTIONS EXPERT AND NATURAL LEADER, JEAN HAS THE INSTINCTS AND KNOW-HOW TO DRIVE YOUR BUSINESS FORWARD. GET IN TOUCH WITH HER TO FIND OUT WHAT SHE CAN DO FOR YOU.

GET IN TOUCH WITH JEAN
✉ JEAN.DENNISTON@GMAIL.COM

117

Why This Works

This candidate's infographic resume has a branding statement that clearly spells out her forte, and the brands she has been affiliated with appear immediately below to connect the message. The area graph shows, in measurable terms, the impact her work has had for clients. This resume, like the others, includes a statement about her unique attributes in terms that an employer would value. (See Figure 6-4.)

LINDSEY JULIAN
She's a leader. A go-getter. Social media savvy.

Lindsey's got the brand experience, flexibility, and organizational skills it takes to deliver what clients need right when they need it. With her finger on the pulse of what's happening, she'll find the trends your clients need to know about to make sure they're launching the best campaigns out there today. Whatever the challenge, she's got the ability and drive to get it done, do it right, and make it count.

JOB HISTORY + CAREER HIGHLIGHTS

2012–present
Account Coordinator

StudioGood Digital Marketing Agency
Identifies client needs and delivers solutions. Ensures that deadlines and deliverables are met on time and within budget. Collaborates in creative and developmental strategic planning sessions. Oversees multiple accounts and editorial calendars. Manages clients' social accounts. Tracks social media metrics and identifies trends to find new ways to engage with users.

2011–2012
Writing Tutor

University Writing Center, California Polytechnic State University San Luis Obispo
Worked one-on-one with students to edit and revise papers for grammar and clarity.

2011
Public Relations and Marketing Intern
A French Touch Parisian Skincare Salon
Organized and promoted store events with responsibilities ranging from budgeting to scheduling to event marketing. Created bi-weekly and monthly blog content, promotional videos, press releases, and newsletters.

2011
Marketing Intern
Get the Word Out Brand Communication
Developed editorial content calendars and creative marketing strategy.

WHAT THEY SAY

"It is an absolute pleasure to work with Lindsey. She's bright, hardworking, and always keeps her projects on track. Her work ethic rivals anyone's I have seen throughout my career. Her drive is unwavering."

Katy McGrath **Account Director, StudioGood Digital Marketing Agency**

"Lindsey is extremely talented with long-term project planning because she pays close attention to detail. She lets nothing get past her. Her senior project on social media and brand loyalty was one of the strongest presentations I've seen in recent years."

Dr. Dan Eller **Professor of Public Relations, Cal Poly State University**

"Lindsey created an individualized approach for each of her students at the writing center. She's an extraordinary teacher and communicator with an exceptional ability to figure out what people are trying to say and help them to express it more clearly."

Dawn Janke **Cal Poly Writing & Rhetoric Center**

EDUCATION

2011
BS, Journalism with Public Relations Concentration
California Polytechnic State University, San Luis Obispo

THE SOCIAL VOICE BEHIND THE BRANDS

BY THE NUMBERS

How have her clients' social accounts grown in the past month?

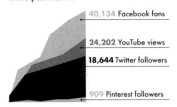

40,134 Facebook fans

24,202 YouTube views

18,644 Twitter followers

909 Pinterest followers

Her social media expertise includes…

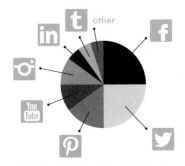

GET IN TOUCH

Email: lindseyjulian3@gmail.com
Phone: 805.297.0293
Twitter: lindseyjulian3

FIGURE 6-4 **Digital Marketing Professional**

Why This Works

This two-page infographic resume entices readers to see what is on the second page, and they'll be glad they did, because this is where the candidate's measurable accomplishments and awards appear. Company logos and testimonials help this candidate stand apart. An interesting feature of this resume is a skills key that describes key competencies and that also matches up with the work experience so the reader can see where the skills were used and mastered. (See Figure 6-5.)

FIGURE 6-5
IT Professional

120

THE INFOGRAPHIC RESUME

📶 NUMBERS *

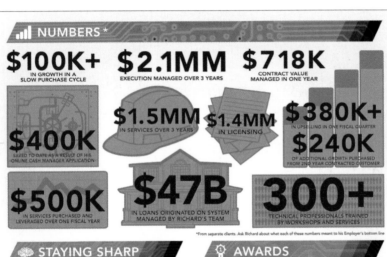

$100K+
IN GROWTH IN A
SLOW PURCHASE CYCLE

$2.1MM
EXECUTION MANAGED OVER 3 YEARS

$718K
CONTRACT VALUE
MANAGED IN ONE YEAR

$1.5MM
IN SERVICES OVER 3 YEARS

$1.4MM
IN LICENSING

$380K+
IN UPSELLING IN ONE FISCAL QUARTER

$400K
SAVED TO DATE AS A RESULT OF HIS
ONLINE CASH MANAGER APPLICATION

$240K
OF ADDITIONAL GROWTH PURCHASED
FROM 2ND YEAR CONTRACTED CUSTOMER

$500K
IN SERVICES PURCHASED AND
LEVERAGED OVER ONE FISCAL YEAR

$47B
IN LOANS ORIGINATED ON SYSTEM
MANAGED BY RICHARD'S TEAM

300+
TECHNICAL PROFESSIONALS TRAINED
BY WORKSHOPS AND SERVICES

*From separate clients. Ask Richard about what each of these numbers meant to his Employer's bottom line

🧠 STAYING SHARP

A life-long learner, Richard makes a point of developing new skills all the time. Here's some of the continuing education courses he's taken recently:

DEVELOPING CUSTOMER RELATIONSHIP SKILLS
TRANSFORMATIONAL LEADERSHIP CONFERENCE
EMPOWERING YOURSELF IN THE 21ST CENTURY
CLOUD STRATEGY AND PLATFORMS
MICROSOFT TECH-READY CONFERENCE
MICROSOFT OPERATIONS ESSENTIALS V4 (MOF)
ITIL V2 & V3 CERTIFIED

♥ GIVING BACK

Richard doesn't stop being a problem solver and leader when the workday ends. Helping people and giving back is how he makes an impact in the business world and how he lives his life.

S.O.N.S. INC.
Outreach and ministry leader organizing and offering food drives, community support services, and clergy services to his community.

🏅 AWARDS

CUSTOMER PARTNER EXPERIENCE AWARD	2013
ACCOLADES FROM ACCOUNT TEAMS AND CUSTOMERS	2012
	2011
KUDOS AWARDS FROM PEERS, LEADERSHIP, AND COLLEAGUES	2010
OFFICER OF THE BANK RECOGNITION, SUNTRUST BANKS	2009
	2008
MANAGEMENT INCENTIVE PROGRAM NOMINEE FOR LEADERSHIP	2007
NATIONAL BLACK DATA PROCESSING ASSOCIATION NOMINEE	2005
3 IBM THANKS! AWARDS	2001
AWARD FOR CUSTOMER SERVICE "ESSENTIAL PIECE OF EIS"	2000
SUNTRUST BANKS EMPLOYEE OF THE YEAR FOR ENTERPRISE TECH INFRASTRUCTURE	1999
PERFORMANCE AND TEAM WORK AWARDS	1998

📇 CONTACT RICHARD JEFFERSON

Combining outstanding communication skills with a keen sense of how to strategically leverage tech solutions for your business, Richard knows how to effectively manage both teams and technology.

📞

💻 RJEFF2001@HOTMAIL.COM

No Two Snowflakes Are Alike

What you will notice is that every resume that Hagan Blount designs is as unique as the individual he is creating the resume for. Blount is averse to templates and points out that if you were creating an advertisement, you wouldn't use a template. Why would you use one for your resume? The practical answer is cost and time. Not everyone can or will invest money in a professionally designed resume. The infographic tools mentioned in Chapter 7 provide enough customization options to give your infographic resume a unique feel without requiring design or technical skills.

CHAPTER 7

Creating Your Own Infographic Resume

You've seen just a small sampling of the thousands of visual and infographic resumes being used today. Now if you are ready to create your own, you will want a quick design overview and steps to help you focus your resume and use the correct tools and images for the job. This chapter will supply resources, tips, and steps to guide you through the process of creating your own visual resume. And in case you don't have all the design software or know-how, this chapter also includes resumes created by pulling information from your LinkedIn profile to easily create a visual illustration of your story.

Design Basics

Most of us didn't go to school for design, but you will want to know just enough to apply good design strategies to your visual resume. Here are the basics of design theory to help give you a foundation for making choices and building out your visual content.

Components of Design

> Rules can be broken—but never ignored.
> —**DAVID JURY,** typographer and author, 2004[1]

Shapes

From ancient pictographs to modern logos, shapes are at the root of design. They are used to establish layouts, create patterns, and build countless elements on the page. With graphics software such as Illustrator, it is easier than ever to create and manipulate shapes, giving designers the freedom to create them at will.

Lines

Lines are used to divide space, direct the eye, and create forms. At the most basic level, straight lines are found in layouts to separate content, such as in magazine, newspaper, and website designs. This can, of course, go much further, with curved, dotted, and zigzag lines used as the defining elements on a page and as the basis for illustrations and graphics. Often, lines will be implied, meaning other elements of design will follow the path of an imaginary line, such as type on a curve.

Color

Color is an interesting element of graphic design because it can be applied to any other element, changing it dramatically. It can be used to make an image stand out, to show linked text on a website, and to evoke emotion. Graphic designers should combine their experience with color with an understanding of color theory.

Color Makes an Impact

Choosing a dominant color for your visual resume can impact the message you are sending. U.S. advertising studies suggest some universal meanings, though colors can mean different things depending on the culture, situation, and industry. As you consider which color to choose, maybe you can catch the attention of your target employer by mimicking the company's dominant color in your visual resume. The other option is to start by selecting a color you like and then see what Entrepreneur.com says the color signifies in the list below:[2]

- **Blue.** Trustworthy, dependable, fiscally responsible, and secure. Serene and universally well liked.
- **Red.** Aggressive, energetic, provocative, and attention grabbing. Also represents danger or indebtedness.
- **Green.** Health, freshness, and serenity. Associated with wealth or prestige or with calming.
- **Yellow.** Optimism, positivism, light, and warmth. Stimulates creative thought and energy.
- **Purple.** Mystery, sophistication, spirituality, and royalty. Lavender evokes nostalgia and sentimentality.
- **Pink.** Energy, youthfulness, fun, and excitement. Dusty pinks appear sentimental. Lighter pinks are more romantic.

125

- **Orange.** Exuberance, fun, and vitality. Gregarious and often childlike.
- **Brown.** Simplicity, durability, and stability. Terracotta can convey an upscale look.
- **Black.** Serious, bold, powerful, and classic. It creates drama and connotes sophistication.
- **White.** Simplicity, cleanliness, and purity.

Color-Combination Tools

There are literally millions of color combinations and varying shades and hues of a single color. Color-combination tools can help you select the right color combination. Once you find the color or color combination, you can use it for your font, section separators, or even the background, but easy does it. All the tools below provide you with the universal color codes and allow you to copy the code into the software program you choose to use.

- **Kuler** (https://kuler.adobe.com/create/color-wheel/). Kuler is a color-theme tool created by Adobe and is one of the premier tools used by graphic designers. If you pick a color you like, Kuler will generate different complementary combinations to help you select the right combination for your work.
- **Color Scheme Designer** (http://colorschemedesigner.com). This online tool provides a similar output to Adobe Kuler but has some interesting ways of generating color themes by allowing you to select single color schemes or complementary multicolored combinations.
- **Mudcube** (http://mudcu.be/sphere/). This color resource not only provides the hex numbers for each color (helpful if using HTML or online site); it also helps you to build up a color scheme from one chosen shade. If you're unsure what color scheme you should be going for, Mudcube provides a selection of themes from a drop-down menu.
- **TinEye** (http://labs.tineye.com/multicolr). This website uses a database of 10 million Creative Commons images from Flickr to let you explore color combinations. If you want to include images

or photographs based on color, this is the tool to use. It may also offer ideas for images to use on your infographic resume.

Typography

Typography is defined by *Merriam-Webster's* as the style, arrangement, or appearance of printed letters on a page. When selecting the typeface (font) for your documents, careful consideration should be given to ensure it conveys the correct message. Your goal is to blend the images, typeface, and layout on the page to engage the reader. Choice of typefaces, size, alignment, color, and spacing all come into play.

Typeface Matters

The type of font you choose to use says a lot about you and more importantly has an impact on how your audience feels about the trustworthiness of the information you are sharing.

Baskerville is the most widely trusted font according to a study conducted by the *New York Times*.[3] In the first part of the study, *New York Times* readers were presented with the same scientific study but in different typefaces: Baskerville, Computer Modern, Georgia, Helvetica, Comic Sans, and Trebuchet. In the second part of the study, a quiz was administered to evaluate whether the *Times's* readers found the study's conclusions believable. Approximately 45,000 people completed the quiz, and the results were evaluated to see which fonts inspired more confidence in the research and which fonts made the information appear less believable. Baskerville was the clear winner, but Computer Modern was close behind. (See Figure 7-1.)

Baskerville
Computer Modern
Georgia
Trebuchet
Helvetica
Comic Sans

FIGURE 7-1
Variety of Fonts
Commonly Used

127

If you aren't a fan of Baskerville, there are thousands of other fonts to choose from. Just open your word processing software, and you'll see your options. If you are looking for more fonts, you can visit Google Fonts (http: www.google.com/fonts) to see the vast collection there.

Art, Illustration, and Photography

A powerful image can make or break a design. Photographs, illustrations, and artwork tell stories, support ideas, and grab the audience's attention. Graphic designers can create this work on their own, or you can commission an artist or photographer, or you can purchase art or photographs through websites. As you create your infographic, think about opportunities to replace text with an icon, logo, or shape or consider adding one next to the text to more clearly emphasize your point.

Clip Art and Icons

If you are creating your infographic from scratch, the resources that follow provide clip art and icons to help spiff up your professional-looking graphics. Some infographic-creating software packages include sets of icons, so be sure to investigate your options.

- **Icons Etc.** (http://icons.mysitemyway.com/). This site offers free icons and clip art stock images for web design, application design, graphic design, and many other purposes. The royalty-free stock icons and stock clip art are free for use in both personal and commercial projects.
- **Iconfinder** (http://www.iconfinder.com). Search for images or icons for your infographics. Some images aren't allowed for commercial use, and some require a back link, so be sure to select the licensing that's appropriate for your use.
- **All-Free-Download.com** (http://all-free-download.com/free-icon/). This site aggregates royalty-free images from other sites to offer thousands of web and social media icon sets, clip art, and photos.

Texture

Texture can refer to the actual surface of a design or to the visual appearance of a design. For the purpose of your infographic resume, rich, layered graphics can create visual texture. Other ways to incorporate texture include background patterns such as wood grain or marble. You could also choose an abstract circuit board as the backdrop for a section of your infographic resume, especially if you are an electrical engineer.

Rules for Creating Great Infographics

Throwing charts and graphs on a wall and hoping they'll stick isn't the best strategy. In order to create a great infographic, you'll want to make sure that the information you share is important to the reader and that you select an appropriate image to simplify what the data or information means.

Planning Your Infographic

Hagan Blount, who creates infographic resumes, suggests you ask yourself a few questions when you're designing your infographic resume:

> Number one, if you raised a metric X percent over X years, is that substantial in the eyes of the reader? If it may or may not be, can you define it as such? Can you speak about it substantively in an interview? Number two, does it reduce the amount of time the reader has to spend looking for the most important part of your resume? Will this particular graphic take more than one aspect of your performance into account? Number three, do you want to do it for the next company? If you're not excited about doing this for the next company, don't include it. If it meets all three criteria, you've got a salient component to your infographic resume.

129

You may find it helpful to reference the material in Chapter 3, "Telling the Story of You," to help you associate numbers and images with each one of your skills and accomplishments.

Gather Ideas from Other Infographics

This book offers many examples, but they are only a snapshot of the thousands of different ways to visually show complex data. If you would like to see other infographics to gain ideas, the following list offers some sites you can investigate. In researching resumes for this book, many of these sites were valuable. You can conduct a search using the terms *visual resume, infographic cv,* or *infographic.* You can even search Google Images by searching for *"resume + infographic"* or replace the word *resume* with any other key word or topic you are interested in finding infographics about.

- **Cool Infographics** (http://www.coolinfographics.com)
- **Daily Infographic** (http://dailyinfographic.com)
- **Huffington Post's Infographics** (http://www.huffingtonpost.com/news/infographics/)
- **Information Is Beautiful** (http://www.informationisbeautiful.net)
- **Mashable Infographics** (http://mashable.com/category/mashable-infographics/)
- **Pinterest** (http://www.pinterest.com)
- **Visual.ly** (http://visual.ly)

Choose the Best Infographic Elements

You don't have to use every type of chart or graph, but you could. Each of these charts conveys information differently. To get an idea of how many options you have available to you, just open up Microsoft Excel, Word, or PowerPoint and see how many different types of charts are available. You may also have ideas based on some of the sample infographic resumes featured in Chapters 5 and 6.

- **Pie charts** help show percentage or proportional data; in other words, they show the composition of a data element, such as what job skills you use in a typical day. Pie charts work best when displaying a limited number of categories. When there are too many categories, it is difficult for the eye to distinguish between the relative sizes of the different slices, and so the chart becomes difficult to interpret. Show each section with different colors or shades to improve readability. (See Figure 7-2.)

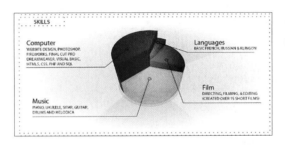

FIGURE 7-2
Pie Chart
Pie chart from Jason Toff's resume

- **Bar graphs** display data such as amounts, characteristics, times, and frequency. A bar graph displays information in a way that quickly and easily helps viewers make generalizations and draw conclusions. An increase in company sales and other cumulative measurements are good data to use. The bars can run horizontally or vertically. (See Figure 7-3.)

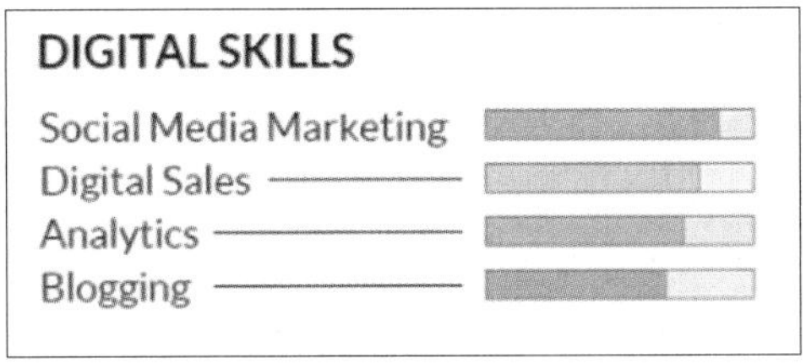

DIGITAL SKILLS

Social Media Marketing
Digital Sales
Analytics
Blogging

FIGURE 7-3
Bar Graph
Bar graph from Kyle Bahr's resume

131

- **Line graphs and area graphs** are used to track changes and show data trends over time. Your work history, skill development, or growth in knowledge would make good examples. (See Figures 7-4 and 7-5.)

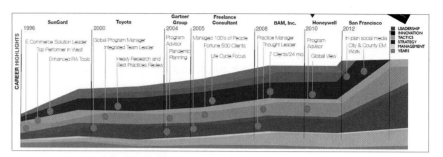

FIGURE 7-4
Line Graph
Line and area graph from Kevin Burton's resume

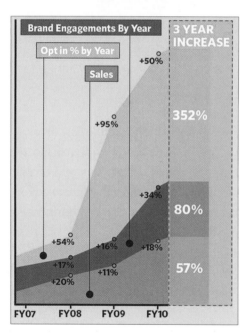

FIGURE 7-5
Area Graph
Area graph from Daniel Brienza's resume

- **Pictographs or ideograms** organize and show information using quantities of small pictures in a chart to represent frequency or quantity. (See Figure 7-6.)

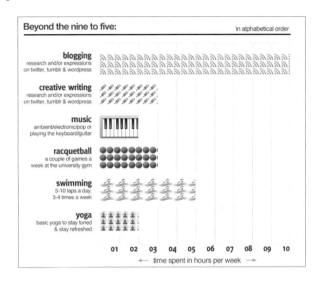

FIGURE 7-6
Pictograph
Pictograph from
Sneha Kochak's
resume

You can make all these graphs using Microsoft chart tools and save the chart or graph by right-clicking on the image, selecting *save as*, and choosing the .jpeg option.

Create Your Own Word Cloud

Copy and paste any text into one of the word-cloud generators listed below, and you can create your own visualization of keywords. The larger the word, the more frequently it appears in the text you've pasted. You could copy the text from your resume, LinkedIn profile, or recommendations, and type in the keywords you want to highlight.

- **Tagcrowd** (http://tagcrowd.com)
- **Tagul** (http://tagul.com)
- **Tagxedo** (http://www.tagxedo.com)
- **Wordle** (http://www.wordle.net)

Stats or Key Facts

Simplify important accomplishments or quantify significant numbers by listing a large number and a few words to describe what the number represents. (See Figure 7-7.)

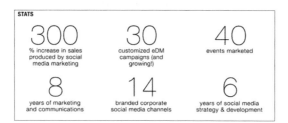

STATS

300
% increase in sales produced by social media marketing

30
customized eDM campaigns (and growing!)

40
events marketed

8
years of marketing and communications

14
branded corporate social media channels

6
years of social media strategy & development

FIGURE 7-7
Key Facts
Stats from Brad Crabtree's resume

Quotes

A quote could be a customer testimonial, manager recommendation, or even your favorite professional quote. Quotes also offer a form of social proof—evidence that other people endorse the work you do.

QR Code Generator

Several infographic resume samples use QR, or Quick Response, codes. In the mobile world we live in today, providing easy access to information on demand can help set you apart. A QR code is scanned using the camera on a mobile device that then links to and opens the data you've specified on the device. You could link to your contact information, LinkedIn profile, visual resume, or even standard text resume.

QR codes would be particularly helpful when you are on the go, for example when attending a career fair, conference, or even a networking meeting. Listed below are two free sites that will convert the information you specify into your own QR code. Just add the information you wish to include, such as your name, phone number, e-mail address, or website URL, and the software will create a code you can put on business cards or resumes. The QR code offers a convenient way to share your contact information in a vCard format that allows the person scanning the code to save the information into a smartphone.

- **QReate & Track** (http://app.qreateandtrack.com/#/create/url)
- **XZing** (http://zxing.appspot.com/generator/)

In order to read a QR code, your mobile device (with a camera) needs a QR code reader. Here are some recommendations, or you can go to the app store on your phone and select one.

- **I-nigma** (http://www.i-nigma.com). Android, iPhone, and Windows Phone versions
- **RedLaser** (http://redlaser.com/). Android, iPhone, and Windows Phone versions
- **Scan** (http://scan.me/). Android, iPhone, and Windows Phone versions

Tools to Create Infographics

Now that you've got some ideas of what to include, you are ready to start creating your infographic. If you have design skills and a program like Adobe InDesign or Illustrator, you are ready to go. You could even use Microsoft PowerPoint to create an infographic by changing the size of the page. But if you are looking for something better and geared specifically toward creating infographics, there are numerous free and low-cost online tools available. Here are some of the top recommendations and key features to help you design your own infographic resume.

- **Piktochart** (http://Piktochart.com) is a site specifically built for creating infographics. As a free user, you have access to seven themes branded with the Piktochart name in the footer. You can upgrade your membership to remove the branding and gain access to 100+ templates, starting at $14 a month. One theme titled "Apropos" is specifically designed to feature a personal infographic about your experience. Each template comes complete with hundreds of icons representing agriculture, education, entertainment, food and beverage, geography, people, social media, shapes, sports, and transportation. You can also add images from Piktochart's collection or clip art–like illustrations. You can choose images from education, entertainment, layered background, or shapes. If you have a headshot or photos or images you would like to use, you can upload five images into the infographic for free. If you would like to add charts, simply drag and drop the charts icon into the template you are working on. Just enter the data and select the best chart, and it shows up in your project.

- **Infogr.am** (http://infogr.am) walks you through the steps for creating free interactive charts and infographics. Start by selecting one of the five free templates with different color schemes. From here you can add different modules: charts, text, maps, pictures, or video. There are 30 different types of charts, ranging from the traditional bar charts to pictorial charts from a word cloud to a tree map to add variety to your infographic. The text option allows you to create a quote, facts or figures, or timer module as well as headlines and chart titles. The free version does not allow you to download the published infographic, but it does create a public link you can share with your social networks. You could even embed your infographic into your LinkedIn profile.

- **Easel.ly** (http://www.easel.ly) provides 15 templates to get you started designing an infographic. Before you select the template, be sure it has the right elements or types of charts. Easel.ly does not offer any charts in its menu options at this time. The categories of images or artwork to choose from include animals, banners, food, icons, landmarks, maps, music, nature, people, and transportation. You may be limited in your options based on the available components of the vheme you select. You can drag and drop different shapes, graphs, pictorials, and text boxes, or you can upload your own images onto the canvas or into your project. The finished product can be downloaded, or the URL can be shared with your social networks.

Infographic Resume Applications

Sometimes taking on the task of learning one more thing is more than you can handle. You are in luck. This section features some easy work-arounds to help you get the eye-catching infographic resume you desire and doesn't require any design skills. These applications convert information from your LinkedIn profile into an infographic resume.

- **Kinzaa** (kinzaa.com). With Kinzaa you can create your info-graphic resume based on information imported from your LinkedIn profile, or if you prefer, you can manually enter your own information. This site lets you upload video and specify the primary skills used in each job you list. A graphic timeline introduces the work history. There is an extensive section of charts at the end that highlight work style and personality traits as well as preferred working environment. Your resume can also be downloaded as a pdf to make it easy for a recruiter or hiring manager to obtain a hard copy. (See Figure 7-8.)

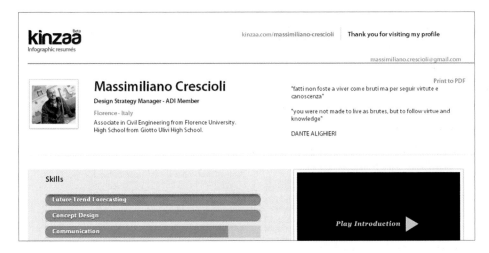

FIGURE 7-8
Concept Design Professional
http://bit.ly/1m0OuiT

- **Visual.ly** (http://www.KellyServices.com/resumebuilder). Visual.ly and Kelly Services, an employment agency and recruitment company, partnered to help you create an infographic resume based on information from your LinkedIn profile. This is a free service. Using the data from your LinkedIn profile, you can create a visually appealing overview of key information from your LinkedIn profile. You can choose from one of five templates, which emphasize different parts of your work history. Some templates pull in a single LinkedIn recommendation; other templates focus on years of experience and skills. Before your select your template, think about your strongest assets and be sure the template you select draws attention to them. You do not have the ability to edit or move elements around within your infographic. You do have the ability to download a pdf version of the document and can share a link to your resume across your social networks. (See Figures 7-9 and 7-10.)

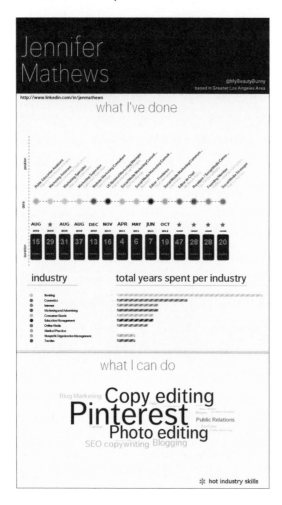

FIGURE 7-9
Social Media Strategist, Copy Editor, Blogger
http://bit.ly /1gFQdWQ

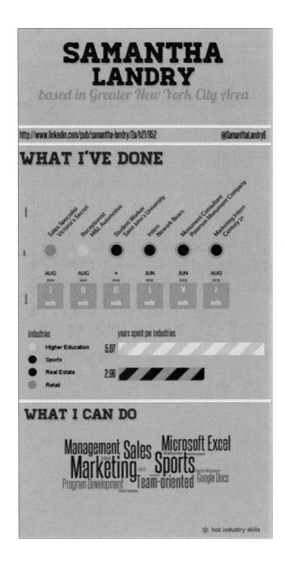

FIGURE 7-10
Marketing Professional
http://bit.ly/1a4u3Pw

Why These Work

These infographic resumes summarize industry experience, key skills, work timeline, word clouds, and a recommendation from one of the resume's connections to help showcase valuable information without a lot of effort because the information is pulled from your LinkedIn profile. (See Figure 7-10.)

- **ResumUp** (http://resumup.com). This tool visually maps out your work history, skills, and other key components of your career.

ResumUp creates your infographic resume by using the professional information in your Facebook or LinkedIn account. There are many optional sections you can add or hide. Adding skills, hobbies, identity, or traits, as well as Klout scores, allows you to deliver more insight about you to recruiters and employers. There is no cost to set up your profile. ResumUp also has a second feature that encourages you to set future goals and maps out exactly what roles you need to get there and who, in your network, can be a source of information or advice.

Why This Works

A horizontal layout gives ample room for Christopher Cribb to convey his work history, industries he has worked in, key skills, personality traits, interests, and more. It uses primary colors to illustrate work history, and red font and icons help attract attention to important aspects of his qualifications. This resume includes his desired occupation and clearly spells out that he is not willing to relocate. Its landscape layout also steps away from the up-and-down orientation of the traditional resume format. (See Figure 7-11.)

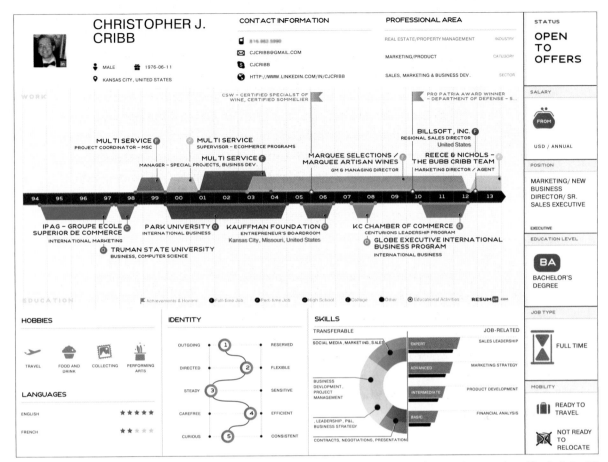

FIGURE 7-11 **New Business Director** http://bit.ly/1iSapVF

- **Beyond.com** (http://www.beyond.com). Create your Career Portfolio, which serves as a visually informative snapshot of your career by mapping accomplishments into a timeline. By connecting your LinkedIn account, the tool can convert a majority of your information into your infographic resume. The top section of the document defines your goals and summarizes your experience, and it can include links to social media outlets. The resume can include a timeline graphic, photo, word cloud, and interests outside of work and subtly uses icons to mark the different sections of the resume. A print option and option to directly message the resume owner are additional features that set this infographic resume apart. There is no charge to use this tool for members of the free Beyond community.

Advice to Ponder

"I think that if you're going to go it alone and make your own infographic resume," says Hagan Blount, "the compelling story is just as important as the good design. If you're not able to really boil down all of your skills into why you'd be perfect for this next job, you are going to have a bigger issue than if the design is not quite on point. We are in the age of the storytellers. If you can tell a clear, concise, and interesting story in a few paragraphs, leaving the reader captivated and clamoring for more, that's how you get the interview. In the end, that's the only thing this document is supposed to do."

CHAPTER 8

Don't Overlook LinkedIn

With all this talk about resumes, do you think you can bypass LinkedIn? Absolutely not! Recent studies report more than 90 percent of employers are turning to LinkedIn.[1] This means that almost every employer is using LinkedIn to search for talent, not just post jobs. Posting jobs results in hundreds of applications, and about half of the applicants won't be qualified.[2] Time constraints may prevent recruiters from reviewing your online presence, but according to Jobvite, a company that develops tools for social recruiting and applicant tracking, 78 percent of recruiters have actually hired through a social network, and 92 percent of those recruiters hired people they found on LinkedIn.[3]

You will need a LinkedIn profile, and it needs to correlate to your resume, though it doesn't have to match word for word. In fact, your LinkedIn profile should fill in the blanks and provide more insight. Readers should learn more about you than what they might find on your resume. Your profile should provide a sense of your work ethic, work values, and motivation. This chapter is filled with ways you can amp up your LinkedIn profile and give it the power of a portfolio.

Turn Your LinkedIn Profile into a Portfolio

Your LinkedIn profile is more than just a boring online resume. Your challenge is to think like a marketer in a big name brand such as Coke, Ford, or the *New York Times* and use video, presentations, and images to convey your message. Company websites and commercials contain customer testimonials, product demonstrations, and visual proof of their products. Companies are doing much more than stagnant print advertising, and with the power of the Internet, so can you!

To make your LinkedIn profile function like a portfolio, you'll want to add pictures, slide shows, work samples, and links to articles mentioning you. LinkedIn calls this embedding media, and this feature began rolling mid-2013.[4]

144

What Media Can I Add?

LinkedIn says it officially supports images, video, audio, presentations, and documents by certain providers. This will allow you to share content from these providers that will be viewable from within the LinkedIn application. You can see a list of the providers at http://help.linkedin.com/app/answers/detail/a_id/34327.

LinkedIn lets you easily embed your work from the sites listed below into your profile. If you create accounts and upload your presentations or work to these popular web-based sharing applications first, you will simplify the integration with LinkedIn. And if you aren't familiar with these applications, they might be worth your time to check out.

PRESENTATIONS AND DOCUMENTS

- Prezi
- Scribd
- SlideShare

OTHER

- Behance
- Issuu
- Kickstarter
- Quantcast

If you plan to upload a file from your computer into your profile, note these specifications for file types and size:[5]

- **File size:** Not to exceed 100 MB
- **Presentations:** .pdf, .ppt, .pps, .pptx, .ppsx, .pot, .potx, .odp
- **Documents:** .pdf, .doc, .docx, .rtf, .odt
- **Images:** .png, .gif, .jpg, .jpeg

Naming Your Embedded Files

A little common sense and SEO (search engine optimization) applies when uploading files. You want your audience to understand what the file contains, so name the upload clearly. If the file or link contains

145

your resume, instead of naming it "my resume.doc," use "your name resume.doc" or better yet "your name job title resume.doc." This is true for any social network or portfolio site you may decide to use to share documents. The SEO strategy here is that you would want all the files and references to your name to appear in search results if a recruiter, or anyone else, searches for your name.

Where to Put Embedded Media

Embedded media content can upload with the image to the bottom of your summary section. You can also upload or link to media within each position listed in your experience section. And finally, you can upload media files or links in your education section. Just look for the little blue box, which indicates you can insert media.

What to Showcase

Think about the problems you've solved at work, not your daily job duties. What differentiates you from the hundreds and thousands of other people who have the same job title as you? In Chapter 3, there were some brainstorming questions to help you create accomplishment stories. Think about visual proof for any of those accomplishments. Is there a picture of you receiving an award? Have you given a presentation or spoken at a conference? Have you written articles? Do you have recent certifications?

What would you want people to find if they searched and found your LinkedIn profile? These are the images, articles, and content you can create and publish yourself online through one of the applications listed above. Think of your LinkedIn profile as a brag book, and please, begin collecting screenshots, photos, and links today. Here are some other ideas of content you can include in your presentation or media links:

- **Letters of recommendation.** You have probably received letters of recommendation or testimonials from past customers. Why not create a presentation featuring these quotes? Just be sure to ask permission to use the quotes or testimonials from the people who have written them. And by the way, this is a great opportunity to reestablish your connection with these people. You will notice testimonials in many of the sample resumes provided; some can even be copied and pasted directly from LinkedIn.

- **Work samples.** You may have created reports, work instructions, work-flow diagrams, and other content as an output of projects you worked on. While you may not be able to use the actual documents, you could create a mock-up to share. You can upload and publish documents into SlideShare and then embed the link into either the summary, work experience, or education section of your LinkedIn profile.

- **Video.** Everyone may not be comfortable in front of a camera, but the video doesn't have to show your face. It could be a "how-to" video. For example, you could create a video on how to create pivot tables, or how to create project plans, or how to organize your e-mail. Use screen casting tools to record your demonstration and upload it to YouTube. Just remember to keep it short. Most ads run under three minutes. Other video ideas might include showcasing photos or images. Animoto.com can turn photos into a 30-second video and publish it to the web for free.

I've Got Nothing

If you don't have anything, create it! You can create a presentation highlighting your accomplishments and publish it to SlideShare. This is fairly simple to do. The most difficult part of the process is figuring out how you will tell your story in a compelling manner and capture the heart and mind of the recruiter with your presentation. You will find tips in Chapter 10 to help with the planning process. Search SlideShare and get ideas from other users who have created online resumes or personal presentations.

LinkedIn Profile Checklist

The suggestions in the sections below should help you get maximum impact from every square inch of space on your profile. Even more importantly, many of these suggestions will help your profile show up in search results. TheLadders conducted another eye-tracking survey

147

of 30 recruiters, this time evaluating where they looked on LinkedIn profiles. What the heat map showed was that recruiters spent 19 percent of the total time on profiles looking at the picture. Next, recruiters looked at the current job position and education, and finally, minimal time was spent looking at skills, specialties, or older work experiences.[6]

Headline

Your profile headline is the first thing someone sees after your name. It should help the reader understand the role you want to do next and contain keywords important to your future profession.

Photo

Choose a professional, high-quality headshot for your photograph. Consult Chapter 3 if you need a reminder about the definition of a good headshot.

E-mail

List all your e-mail addresses so they are associated with your LinkedIn profile. You can set the default e-mail, which will be viewable by your connections and the account that receives InMail and updates from LinkedIn.

Vanity URL

Your LinkedIn profile has a URL that, by default, LinkedIn assigns with letters and numbers. When you view your profile in edit mode, your vanity URL looks something like this: www.linkedin.com/pub/jim-doe/33/44b/442. You can and should edit this by adding your name (www.linkedin.com/in/yourname). Changing this URL will help people find you, and it also looks more professional when you include it on your resume, business card, and e-mail signature.

Other Web References

If you have a personal website, professional Twitter account, or links elsewhere on the web, you can add them to your profile within the contact info section at the top. You should change the label from "other" to a short, descriptive title.

Summary

Consider this section a mini bio. Highlight the best of your background, experience, and skills. You could also provide insight into your leadership style, personality, values, longer-term goals, or outside interests. Keep the reader's attention by using short paragraphs. One way to make it more personal is by writing in the first person by using "I," "me," or "my." You may want to include your e-mail address in this section to make it easy for people who are not connected to contact you. Consider including interests, stories, and examples of your work to help the reader understand what makes you tick.

Work Experience

List all the significant work history and include strong, keyword-rich descriptions and accomplishments under each position. Your work experience should be very similar to what is listed on your resume.

Embed Media

Add media (documents, video, images, and audio) to your profile to make it an online portfolio. You can embed these links in your summary, work experience, and education sections.

Skills and Endorsements

List all the skills and areas of expertise that are most important to your profession and that you want to highlight. You can list as many as 50. You will learn more about endorsements later in this chapter.

Education

Include all the institutions you attended. List your concentration, major, and minor. If you are a recent graduate, include clubs, committees, and groups you were active in.

Certifications, Test Scores, and Courses

These sections are particularly helpful for new graduates. List the most relevant and important information. Use these sections to highlight recent acquisition of knowledge through coursework since this information is also valuable in the eyes of recruiters.

Projects

You can reference class projects, special work assignments, and side gigs as a project. You could even add your professional reading list as a career development project. This is another way to showcase skills and experience.

Recommendations

Ask for recommendations from colleagues, managers, or even clients who know your work. Writing recommendations can be difficult and time consuming. You can help simplify the request for a recommendation by providing some ideas about the projects you worked on together or the skills you want to highlight.

Honors and Awards, Publications, and Patents

Complete these sections with as much detail as necessary to show your skills. Instead of just listing the award, describe what you did to earn it. Include details about the publication or patent in order to help the reader understand what knowledge you have in certain areas.

Organizations, Volunteering, and Causes

Provide details about your involvement in professional associations and the organizations you belong to or committees you serve on. You may also choose to list the volunteer work you do and causes you support. Use discretion when choosing to include any religious or political affiliations.

Personal Details

Your birth date and marital status are the least important details within this section. You may choose not to include this information on your profile.

Make It Complete

Don't leave information blank or overlook details that may help set you apart such as languages, honors and awards, patents, courses, test scores, certifications, volunteering and causes, organizations, and interests.

Make It Public

By default, LinkedIn sets your profile to be viewable to the public. For active job seekers this is the best option.

Special Sections for College Students and Recent Graduates

These sections are particularly helpful for college students. They give you the opportunity to highlight accomplishments outside of a formal job or work assignment.

- **Courses.** List select courses on your profile, especially those that qualify you for positions you are seeking.
- **Projects.** Participating in projects shows the ability to apply classroom learning to real-world challenges and work effectively as part of a team. Include projects that demonstrate experience relevant to your professional goals.
- **Honors & awards.** In this section, you can provide objective validation for your accomplishments. Be sure to list dean's list, merit-based scholarships, and other recognition.
- **Organizations & causes.** List your contributions outside the classroom through participation in on-campus or external organizations. Your involvement conveys commitment to an activity or interest and can even show leadership abilities.
- **Test scores.** If you have excelled at standardized tests or have a stellar GPA, include these results on your profile. Some employers may view strong test scores as indicators of good problem-solving skills.

How to Get the Most Out of LinkedIn

Endorsements

LinkedIn's endorsements feature allows you to endorse people in your network for their skills and expertise. According to LinkedIn, endorsements help boost the strength of your profile, and they increase the likelihood you'll be discovered for opportunities related

151

to the skills your connections endorsed. The verdict is still out by many LinkedIn gurus on this feature's usefulness, but you should know about it! Endorsements provide a simple, quick way for people you know to give your work skills a thumbs-up. Likewise, you can do the same for others. Be thoughtful and purposeful in whom you choose to endorse for what skills. In other words, don't go on an endorsing rampage. Endorse people you honestly know possess the skills you endorse. And some experts believe you should only endorse the skills you have seen in action! Ultimately it is your decision.

Share What You Know in Group Discussions

Groups are an underutilized resource for building brand awareness about you! LinkedIn has groups for professional associations, school alumni, alumni groups from past employers, regional- and city-specific groups, and literally hundreds of other categories. There are even job-seeker groups. You can belong to as many as 50 groups. But more importantly, be strategic and selective and *engage*! Use these groups to build relationships with new people as well as share your content or ideas.

Follow Companies

If there are companies you would like to work for, follow them on LinkedIn. When you follow companies, you can see their company profile updates in your home feed of updates.

Check out the company's insights tab. You will see a list of companies viewed by other LinkedIn users. It says: "People who looked at [company] also viewed:" These listed companies could be competitors or be in the same industry, and they may have similar job opportunities for you to explore.

Part of your regular routine is to monitor the updates of companies you are following.

Applying for Jobs Through LinkedIn

Employers do post jobs on LinkedIn. You can search for jobs, or you may set notifications to receive jobs that may be of interest. To apply for a job posted on LinkedIn, the employer has specified how it wants you to apply—either using your LinkedIn profile or applying directly through the employment portal on the website.

More Ways to Get More from LinkedIn

Keep Up with Industry News

What publications or news sources do you regularly read? This can sometimes be overwhelming. You can use the news-feed settings within LinkedIn to keep up with what's happening in your industry. Take a minute and select the type of news you are interested in keeping up with on your home page by going to Pulse (https://www .linkedin.com/today/). Once you've set your preferences, you'll see top stories when you log in. Armed with current industry news, you can share it among your peers and connections.

Who's Influencing You

One of LinkedIn's features is called "Influencers," which allows you to follow key industry movers and shakers to keep up with what they're saying and sharing. You don't need to be connected to these influencers in order for the articles they write to hit your home page on LinkedIn.

Connect with People

People define their LinkedIn connections differently. LIONs (LinkedIn Open Networkers) generally connect with anyone. At the other end of the spectrum are LinkedIn users who only connect with people they know well. And then there are those who fall in between. Your connections should represent your real-life network. Grow your connections purposefully by inviting people you know first. When you reach out to people you would like to know, personalize the invitations you send and provide a reason for them to want to connect with you.

Be aware of whom you're connected to on LinkedIn. For example, if you're thinking of changing jobs and are connected to your manager and current work colleagues, be aware that they can see your

153

activities and updates. Each time you connect with someone new or make changes to your LinkedIn profile, these activity updates are visible to your network (unless you choose to turn this function off in your settings).

Keep in Touch

People move around from job to job more often today than years ago. LinkedIn makes it much easier to find past colleagues and stay in touch. Make sure you have listed each of your previous employers so that you can connect with past colleagues on LinkedIn. And don't just stop there. You can like or comment on their status update. Or better yet, connect with them in person or by phone once in awhile. It will be much easier to reach out when you need help looking for a job if you keep in touch.

Write Recommendations

Endorsements enable you to write a recommendation for people in your network. Your name and a link to your profile appear on their endorsement page, and your written recommendation appears on your LinkedIn profile as well. When you write a recommendation (either solicited or unsolicited), it shows your support for the person's work as well as demonstrates your communication and leadership capabilities.

Reconsider How You Use LinkedIn

LinkedIn is a multifaceted tool, one that provides you the opportunity to create a positive self-image, keeps you connected, and helps you stay up-to-date on current trends. Rethink how you use it or expand how you are using it. Think about its long-term value to you and your career. Keep building your network, and for the best results, make it mutually beneficial.

Sample LinkedIn Profiles

Your LinkedIn profile should tell your story in words and pictures. Creating a vibrant profile is your opportunity to stand out online and showcase your uniqueness. The following profiles highlight skills, values, and interests that differentiate these people from others who may do similar types of work. (See Figures 8-1 and 8-2.)

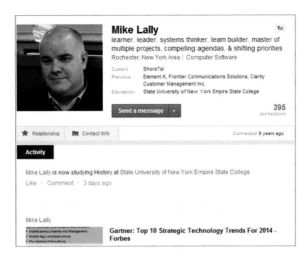

FIGURE 8-1
A Learner, Leader, and Systems Thinker

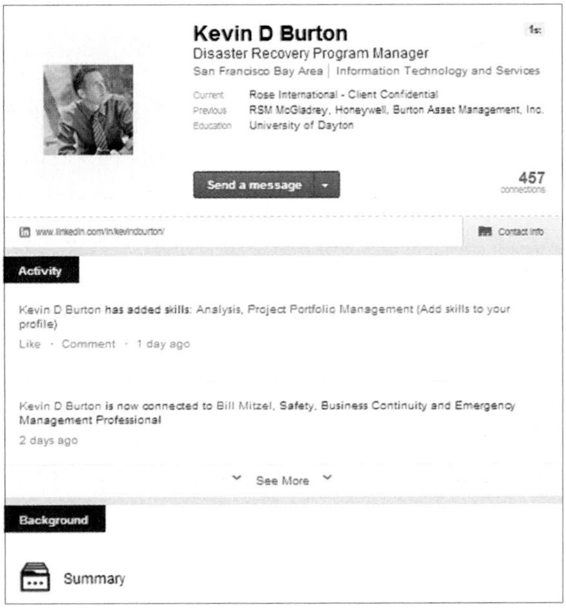

FIGURE 8-2
Disaster Recovery Professional

One Final Word of Caution: There Are Few Absolutes

Every individual on LinkedIn has a different interpretation of how to use the tool. Establish goals for how you plan to use LinkedIn both as a job seeker and as someone who is truly managing his or her career. Always keep in mind standard business etiquette—be polite, considerate, and respectful of differing opinions and views.

CHAPTER 9

Social Resumes

A social resume is a little bit social and a little bit resume. Consider a social resume a real-time view of your online performance. It demonstrates your knowledge, expertise, and interests, but not in the static way an old-fashioned resume would. Employers already research you online because they want to gain more insight into who you are and what's important to you. One way they can infer this information is from reading your status updates, blog posts, portfolio of work, or whatever else Google turns up. A social resume offers you the opportunity to place front and center the posts, images, and content you want to showcase, as well as a way to indicate how and with whom you communicate online. Remember, there is very little that stays private online. This means you will want to pay attention to which social network sites you link to and ensure the content and messages you share align with your future career move.

Consider your social resume a landing page—think of it as a single destination for someone to learn more about you through your prominently featured links to other Internet outlets, such as social networks. It contains a mini bio, which you write, and icons to other destinations; and in many cases, it includes the actual stream of updates from your social networks. A social resume makes it simple for someone to see your profiles and real-time stream of updates on Twitter, Google+, LinkedIn, blogs, or other places you are active online. You control the links you want to showcase. Your social resume helps establishes credibility. If you want to prove you are knowledgeable on the newest sales strategies, you could participate in Twitter chats dedicated to sales professionals and share articles on the subject on LinkedIn. This provides actual proof that you are up on the topic. Your social network updates create a modern-day resume. When you aggregate your profiles and feeds on a single page, you make it easier for people to learn about you. You want recruiters and hiring managers to easily see you are sharing the right content, which is important based on the results of Jobvite's 2013 Social Recruiting Survey. It reported that 93 percent of recruiters are likely to look at a candidate's social profile.[1] To take this one step further, they are looking at LinkedIn to assess professional experience, length of professional tenure, and specific

158

hard skills. They look at Twitter, Facebook, and Google+ to evaluate cultural fit, industry-related posts, and professional experience.

This chapter includes tools to create social resumes and offers tips on how to use social resumes for increased exposure and awareness.

> ### How would someone get on your radar?
>
> Arie Ball, VP Talent Acquisition, Sodexo, is another one of Glassdoor's Talent Warrior award winners. When asked how someone could get on Ball's radar, she responded, "I tend to notice professionals who are actively engaged in their profession, and contribute in a thoughtful way to discussions. Who can help but notice professionals with a true passion for their work, or for causes they believe in?"[2]

Who Benefits Most?

Given the rise in social recruiting and increase in the number of employers checking out applicants online, everyone benefits from having a social resume. It is digital terrain, a little piece of Internet space to help you establish an online presence that showcases expertise and builds credibility.

Whether you are a new graduate pursuing your first job or a seasoned professional looking for your next great opportunity, a social resume establishes a professional impression.

How to Set Up Social Resumes

As mentioned before, a social resume provides a way to easily acquire additional information about you. It compiles all your outlets on a single page. Setting up your social resume is fairly straightforward, but here are some things you should pay attention to.

159

Don't Be Too Wordy

Few people will read every word on a website. As a matter of fact, a person is only likely to read 20 to 28 percent of the text on a web page.[3] This is according to Jakob Nielsen of the Nielsen Norman Group, a consulting firm conducting research about online content and usability.

When writing your bio for your social resume, always keep in mind whom you are writing for. The people you want to read your bio are either potential employers or clients looking for someone with your skill sets and experience. You can address their needs by incorporating a value proposition or short phrases that tell how you can solve their problems. Better yet, provide an example of a success story that shows how you have solved problems. It is unlikely you will be able to tell your full story in an online bio and keep it short enough. Your bio should function as a teaser to get your audience interested in clicking through and learning more. Inserting your personality to give your readers a taste of your work style or interests can help create a personal connection. You can look at some of the bios later in this chapter and review the information in Chapter 2.

Choosing the Right Name and Handle

Each social profile asks that you create a user name for your account; this is often referred to as a handle. It's important to use the same name consistently across your resume and all your profiles. Don't overlook this small detail. Using a consistent online name will greatly improve the accuracy of search results. As a reminder, the best strategy is to use your first and last name as the account or profile name. If your name isn't available, try using a middle initial or certification after your name. Doing this consistently will help recruiters find the right accounts for you.

Choosing the Right Photo

Some social resumes feature a full-screen image; others require just a small thumbnail image. Before you upload yours, it is good to get ideas from people already using that specific social resume tool. Check out the social resumes and see what types of images or photos other people are using as a background or featured image; also pay attention to the industry or the type of work they perform. Some industries and jobs are more conservative, and your photo should match the style. You will notice some social resumes use photos of the people themselves, others have images that are important to people's individual interests, and some social resumes feature a collage of various images. Be sure that the image you use isn't fuzzy or blurry when uploaded and that you have the rights to use an image or photo. You may want to test different images to see which looks best, and be sure you pay attention to the dimension requirements (minimum and maximum sizes) for the best quality. This also helps ensure the image you use is framed like the original.

Connecting Sites and Content to Your Profile

As mentioned above, you should carefully consider which networks you choose to link to your social resume. More links aren't necessarily better if you aren't demonstrating professionalism on all your listed social networks. If you do choose to link to your personal Facebook page, pay close attention to your public posts and avoid oversharing personal information that may be damaging to your reputation. Also make sure your linked profiles contain a professional image and bio that best showcase your talents.

Social resumes also let you link to URLs. If you have a portfolio or personal website, be sure to include links. Additionally, if there are articles that mention you or you have contributed to, those can be listed. And if you have created other social resumes, you can even link those URLs too.

Link or Post Your Social Resume to Your Website or Online Portfolio

Where is the one place on the web you want people to go to learn most about you? Is it your personal website or your LinkedIn profile? If you include a link to your social resume on either or both of these sites, you've again made it easy for someone to track down your other accounts and profiles. Your about page on your website or portfolio could contain a link to your social resume, or if you choose, you may even be able to map your social resume to appear as a page on your website or portfolio. Usually this requires that you pay a nominal monthly fee to a social resume site provider.

Ways to Share Your Social Resume

One of the most obvious places to include a link to your social resume is in your e-mail signature. A link in your e-mail signature is a perfect opportunity to provide additional information about you. Think about how many e-mails you send out in a day, week, or month, especially while you are campaigning for a new job. Wouldn't you want every one of your e-mail recipients to have access to your social resume? Another obvious place for a link to your social resume is on your resume and in your cover letter.

Referencing your social resume on your LinkedIn profile is another opportunity. There are a couple of different places you can reference your social resume within your LinkedIn profile. First, you could add the social resume's URL to your profile in the contact info section as "other website." Instead of leaving the default title "other website," change that title to something more specific such as "My About.me page," "What I'm saying online," or "Proof I know social media." LinkedIn also accepts images and links in your summary. You can embed a screenshot of your social resume in your summary section. When clicked, make sure it links to your social resume. Review the section of Chapter 8 about embedding visual content in your LinkedIn profile.

Almost every social resume provides you with the option to share it as a status update across major social networks. Let the tool help you broadcast your profile. When the site prompts you to share your social resume, follow the steps. You can always create your own status update, which might say, "I've updated my social resume; check it out here [insert link to your social resume]."

Pinterest is becoming a popular tool, so don't pass up the opportunity to post your visual resume to your pinboard. Pinterest's primary focus is sharing images, so this makes it a perfect platform for broadcasting your visual work.

When you share your social resume across various social networks, more people are likely to see it. It is kind of an advertisement for you. And perhaps your status update, featuring your profile, may just hit the eyes of your future boss.

Proactively Send It to a Potential Employer

Do you want to get on the radar of a recruiter at a target company or catch the attention of a recruiter who just posted a great-looking job? Craft a tweet or status update including the recruiter's name, a link to your social resume, and a reason he or she should check you out. Or you could craft a clever e-mail to the recruiter highlighting why you would make an excellent employee and inviting the recruiter to click on the link to your social resume. It shouldn't matter if the company has current openings or not, good recruiters are always on the lookout for future talent. Do you want proof that reaching out to recruiters will be well received? Glassdoor's Talent Warrior Award honors the year's most innovative and socially savvy recruiters and HR professionals, and every single one of them recommends interacting online either through employer communities or directly.[4]

Fringe Benefits

There are other benefits to having a social resume. Your profile and links demonstrate your technical proficiency, provide evidence of your communication skills, highlight your expertise and interests, and serve as testimony to your relationship building and interpersonal communication savvy. These skills transfer to any job in any company. These are also skills an employer is evaluating during the interview. Providing potential employers with proof of these skills earlier in the screening process can help them assess your fit and may give you a competitive advantage.

It doesn't take much time to set up these social resumes, so you could technically create one using each tool. It is difficult to know which tool will be around months or years from now, so it is a wise idea to diversify your message across multiple sites and keep it fresh or updated. These types of sites often improve functionality, so monitor your account and make sure you fully leverage everything it is capable of doing for you. It is also a wise idea to monitor new tools that enter the game to ensure you've fully staked your digital claim.

Social Resume Sites

In this section, you will find descriptions and samples from four social resume tools. Expect to see more of these platforms in the coming months and years.

About.me

The founders of About.me explain they created the site "so that everyone on the planet could assert their own identity. We wanted to offer everyone more control over how they represent themselves online. At that time, everyone was talking about social media—whether it was Facebook, Twitter or LinkedIn."[5]

Personalizing the look of your page is as simple as adding a cover photo, selecting a font and color, and setting your text in an appropriate location. You can change your privacy settings so that people can easily communicate with you via e-mail. From your dashboard, you can see how many people have visited your About.me page, how many users have liked, or complimented your page, and who they are. If you would like to see the About.me pages for people you are following on Twitter or Facebook, the tool offers that function as well. (See Figures 9-1 to 9-4.)

FIGURE 9-1
Customer Service Leader
http://bit.ly/L0znr9

164

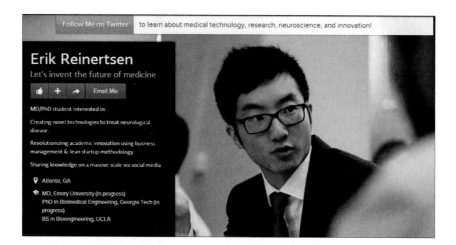

FIGURE 9-4
**MD/PhD
Neuroscience and
Technology**
http://bit.ly/19slNbu

Re.vu

Re.vu displays an infographic of your work history. When you link your LinkedIn profile, Re.vu simply lifts the data and then converts it into infographics. You can add various infographic modules at any point. Re.vu provides you with the option to create sections based on your skills, education, proficiencies, quotes, or personal interests. Of course, you can link to other websites or online content. Re.vu also allows you to add a button so that viewers can e-mail you, and most importantly, you can connect your traditional or text resume so that visitors can download it. Re.vu displays the number of visitors, length of time on page, resume downloads, and number of times you've been contacted from the analytics dashboard. There is no cost to become a user. (See Figures 9-5 to 9-7.)

FIGURE 9-5
Sales Leader
http://bit.ly/1b0bvuh

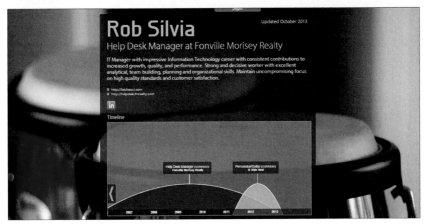

FIGURE 9-6
Help Desk Manager
http://bit.ly /1b0bAOC

Flavors.me

Anyone can make a branded web presence using personal content from around the Internet. Flavors.me offers a handful of different page templates and options to choose from, as well as different color schemes and fonts. Website links and connections to social networks are also included. An added benefit is access to the searchable community of users for you to review more social resume examples and even connect with professionals who have similar career interests. The basic site package is free, with the option to upgrade for $20 a year. The free version does not allow you to see site analytics. (See Figure 9-8.)

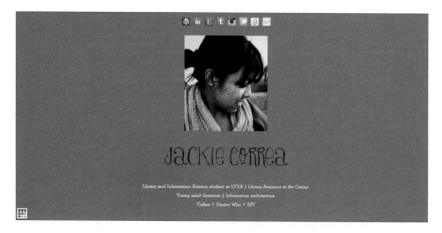

168

Career Cloud's Social Resume

Chris Russell, who founded Career Cloud, has been highly regarded as a job board expert. He founded Allfairfieldcountyjobs.com when job boards were all the rage. Chris follows the hiring trends closely and saw the tide moving toward social recruiting. CareerCloud has several components, one of which is the Social Resume. CareerCloud aggregates posts and status updates from the networks the user chooses to connect to. Chris says it's a home page for your social media activities.

When Chris created his account and began promoting it across LinkedIn, Twitter, Facebook, and his other social networks, he saw a 10 percent increase in new followers and connections across all his accounts. Awareness is the name of the game, and this tool helps put all the social conversations and updates in one place and makes it easier for hiring entities to follow your work across multiple social networks. (See Figure 9-9.)

FIGURE 9-9
Online Recruiting Entrepreneur
http://bit.ly/1kAft6w

169

Claim Your Terrain

As you can see, there is a broad spectrum of industries and occupations represented in these examples. There are many examples of social resumes at all levels and across all fields. Creating a social resume doesn't require a great deal of technical skill, and within a matter of minutes, you have a site to proudly refer people to. And because these sites are somewhat optimized to be search engine friendly and findable, establishing an account on one or more becomes a no-brainer.

CHAPTER 10

Interactive Resumes and Slide Shows

Standing out among a sea of job seekers can be tough, but not impossible. There is still another way to tell your story, show off your skills, and attract an employer's attention.

Job seekers often say, "If I could only get in front of someone, I could prove I'm qualified." A presentation resume could be your chance to prove your qualifications and show your extreme interest in a company or job. This chapter looks at how to craft a presentation that connects you to your audience, provides a list of alternative presentation tools, and shows some examples of job seekers who have used them successfully. Presentations provide just one more alternative for telling your story and pitching you.

Presentations Rock

A presentation provides unlimited opportunities to show your value and your talents. When you craft a presentation using a customized story to fit the needs of a specific employer, it demonstrates your extra effort and interest. This unconventional approach to applying for a job may just capture the recruiter's attention and give you a leg up on the competition. Few job seekers are gutsy enough to attempt this strategy, and this is the very reason you might want to give it a try.

If you are pursuing a career that requires creating or delivering presentations, what better way to sell these skills than by using them to create a presentation. Even if your job may not require presentation skills, creating a presentation resume shows creativity, planning, and the ability to clearly communicate complex data, which may help you stand apart.

How to Get Started

A presentation's purpose is to educate, inform, persuade, motivate, or inspire. As you can see, emotion is a large component of what happens during a presentation. In order for your presentation to evoke emotion, you have to connect with the employer at some level, whether that is having shared values, showcasing your knowledge of the company's products or services, or providing solutions to problems you know the employer needs solved. In short, you want to address the needs of your audience. This isn't a new concept by now; you've seen it throughout the entire book.

Unfortunately, job descriptions don't always provide the level of detail necessary to understand what problems the employer is trying to solve by filling the position. By contacting someone inside the company and researching the company, you may be able to uncover the true needs. Or maybe you can uncover overarching changes that give you some insight, such as the company just landed a contract for new business, it recently downsized, or maybe someone vacated a job suddenly, leaving a gaping hole in the organization. These clues and your previous industry experience can begin to help you understand or predict some of the employer's needs. For example, if there is a new contract, there will be other new employees joining the team, requiring training and leadership. Or the company may need someone with strong project management skills to ensure the on-time delivery of the product. No matter what role you are pursuing, a new contract impacts all parts of the organization, including the one you are interested in filling. If you can demonstrate how you've solved similar challenges, you've already got relevant experience the company may value.

Nancy Duarte is an expert at creating presentations. She has created over a quarter million presentations, including Al Gore's *An Inconvenient Truth*. In one of Nancy's two books on creating winning presentations, *Slide:ology*, she explains that storytelling and images are vitally important to business communication at every level.[1]

> Effective communication is a job requirement now, whether you're trying to beat competitors, communicate vision, demonstrate thought leadership, raise capital, or otherwise change the world. And like it or not, your profession likely requires you to communicate using a visual tool, regardless of your proficiency or training in this medium.

There are five key points Duarte makes about presentations. They include:[2]

- **"Treat your audience as king."** In other words, design slides that meet your audience's needs. Don't just regurgitate your work history and skills because you think you should. Draw the connection based on what is important to your audience.
- **"Spread ideas and move people."** Emotionally connect with your audience. Get people to change how they feel about you and convert their perception of you from stranger to must-meet. You can do this if you truly understand their culture, their needs, their goals, and their mission. Research the company. Better yet, reach out to people who work there and learn about why they like working there, the challenges they are facing, and any other information that will help you truly understand the company.
- **"Help them see what you're saying."** Because half the population is verbal and the other half visual, you will want to incorporate images as well as words. One way you could do this is by using pictures instead of words. A simple way to do this is to substitute logos for the names of companies you have worked for or the school you attended.
- **"Practice design, not decoration."** Minimalistic design philosophy applies here. Less is more. Review each slide and see what you can remove to keep it uncluttered. Duarte says 90 percent of the process is destructive. Also, try not to convey more than one point per slide, but if you must, then just show one point at a time.
- **"Cultivate healthy relationships with your slides—and your audience."** While this advice sounds like it only pertains to live presentations, it also applies to virtual presentations you share. Don't put too much information on a slide or in your presentation. Your purpose is to convince your audience to contact you, not learn everything there is to know about you. Sometimes by leaving out inconsequential information, you can create a teaser and inspire action.

Emulate Great Presenters

If you want your presentation to tell your story in a new way, consider using a more modern storytelling model, known as the three-act structure, which splits your story into three parts: the setup, the confrontation, and the resolution. HubSpot, an inbound marketing software system company, contends that great presenters, like Steve Jobs, prefer to use a "why > how > what" format. In order to do this, begin by answering the one question you know your audience is thinking: "Why should I care?" Your first slide should answer this question. The next set of slides should answer the question "How will this make my life better?" and for the finale, clearly state "What action do I need to take now?"[3]

Your story may sound like this:

Many adult learners feel overwhelmed by the thought of taking online classes. I realize how important it is to develop content that addresses the differing learning styles of adults. As a result, people actually want to sign up for and complete my training. What we've found is that engaged learners bring more ideas back to their teams and improve the overall pool of knowledge for their group. The contagious enthusiasm for the training spreads and grows so that there is demand for the next round of training. I would love to bring this enthusiasm for learning and improved performance outcomes to your company.

When your presentation helps your listeners care about you, they are more likely to view the whole presentation, thereby learning and remembering more. Emotionally connecting with your audience is an idea being tested a lot today by marketers and is based on numerous studies evaluating the correlation between emotions and the impact they have on how long we remember information. The theory is that the stronger the emotional connection during an interaction, presentation, or even commercial, the longer it will be remembered.

175

Start with a Storyboard

Before you jump on your favorite presentation application to create your story or pitch, you will want to map out the story you want to tell. Keep in mind the elements of explanation mentioned in Chapter 3. Some people prefer to create the storyboard on paper; others may be looking for an online template. You can find templates at http://creately.com/diagram-community/popular/t/story-board. These steps, outlined below, should help you put your storyboard together.

Planning

Research and understand the challenges, successes, goals and desires of your audience. Remember, your audience is an employer you want to work for. If you attempt to create a generic storyboard all about you, it is unlikely the viewer will be interested. Your audience is thinking, what's in this for me? Why should I spend my time watching this presentation?

As you map out your storyboard, keep in mind that you will want your first slide to grab the viewers' attention. What you are telling them has to connect and matter to them. In order to accomplish this, create a list of the most important parts of your professional story you want to include: awards, key achievements, promotions, prominent skills, publications. Now, how would your future employer benefit from any or all of these? If you won an award for achieving excellent customer service, how would your future employer benefit? Well, the employer would certainly gain your expertise, but is that all? If the potential employer already has a positive reputation for delivering outstanding customer service, you certainly would fit right in and help the company continue to provide outstanding customer care because it is important to you as well, as illustrated by your award. If you want to take this one step further, you can explain exactly why you care so much about customers. For example, you enjoy helping customers resolve issues because you know how frustrating it can be to feel ignored and that has led you to abandon a company's products in the past. When you take this extra step to try and connect with your potential employer, it shows you share similar values plus serves to emotionally connect with the employer.

Sketching

The next step is to draw out, slide by slide, how you will guide your audience from point A to point B. Each slide represents a single point or idea outlined in the script. It is common to want to put a lot of information on a single slide, but in doing so, you will either overwhelm your audience or lose your audience's attention, or both.

Each slide should contain a strong visual element that relates to the one key point you are making on the slide. Reading slides packed with text is as interesting as reading your resume. Instead of using words, consider using pictures or images that represent your key points, such as company logos, a photograph of you receiving an award, college emblems, or a symbolic image.

Converting to a Presentation

The prework you do will pay out greatly as you begin to convert your sketches into slides. Because you have focus and direction as you create your presentation, you are less likely to worry about what you'll say next, how you'll transition to a new point, or what images you'll use.

Here are some reminders to help your presentation stand out:

- The first slide has to grab people's attention. Make it relevant to your audience.
- Your slide deck needs to be able to stand by itself. You aren't there giving a presentation; it is being viewed independently, which requires your audience to, first, want to invest the time to open your presentation and, second, be compelled to continue to advance through the slides.
- Conclude with a call to action. Tell your viewers what you want them to do after seeing your presentation. Do you want them to contact you? If so, provide several different contact options such as e-mail, phone, and social media accounts.

Find and Use Images

Visual images are critical to telling your story. One option is to use your own high-quality photos, especially if you are a photographer.

177

Another option is to capture screenshots with tools such as Evernote's Skitch, Google Chrome's Screen Capture, Microsoft's Snipping tool, or the built-in functionality within your Mac.

If you are searching for images, you will want to be sure you are using ones that are licensed for use. Creative Commons (CC) is the overseeing entity for image use, and it has established criteria that allow image owners or creators to define how an image can be used. This is called attribution. Understand and follow the terms specified by the image's creator to make sure you can share it publicly. In most cases, you will need to give credit to the owner, which can be done immediately following the image (in your work) or at the end of your work in a section entitled "resources."

There are also images that are in public domain, which means no attribution is necessary. As you search for images, be sure you set your search criteria to find CC-licensed work that is shareable. You can use Flickr or the CC link http://search.creativecommons .org/ to search for usable images, videos, or music files across numerous search engines such as Google's image search, Fotopedia, and more.

If you are really serious about using exactly the right image, you may choose to pay to own the rights to use it. You can browse royalty-free images that you can purchase on iStockphoto or Shutterstock. Expect to pay anywhere from $15 to $100+. These are some popular image collections:

- Getty Images (http://www.gettyimages.com)
- iStockphoto (http://www.istockphoto.com)
- Shutterstock (http://www.shutterstock.com)
- Veer (http://www.veer.com)

Design Elements

The font you choose to use and the color palette also have an impact on your audience. Chapter 7 discussed the important elements of design including suggestions for fonts and colors. If you have already selected fonts and colors for your resume or online portfolio, you may want to consider using the same selections for your presentation.

Consistency can help establish "brand recognition," or more simply put, people may remember your unique style from other material they've seen.

Presentation Tools

If you are looking for some alternatives to the standard Microsoft PowerPoint or Macintosh Keynote, these are some free options:

- **Google Drive Presentation** (https://drive.google.com/). With Google's presentation tool, you can upload your own images and video, add text, and create presentations quickly. You can allow anyone to view or edit your presentation. Existing PowerPoint files can also be uploaded for sharing. Google Drive Presentation is free.
- **Prezi** (http://prezi.com). Prezi is an online presentation tool with both free and paid plans. With any plan you can easily create your own presentations and share them online or download them for offline viewing. With paid plans starting at $59 per year, you get additional features such as the ability to make presentations private and to work offline.
- **PowToon** (http://www.powtoon.com). With PowToon, you can create animated movies and presentations at no cost. The user interface was designed and tested to be as simple as possible for the nontechnical animator. The free version can be upgraded to remove the PowToon watermark and increase movie length from 5 to 15 minutes, plus there are other higher-quality features, starting at $49 a month.
- **SlideShare** (http://www.slideshare.net). SlideShare is another online presentation tool that has both free and paid options. You can't create presentations with SlideShare, but you can upload presentation files. With the free plan, your presentations will include ads, but you will get unlimited uploads. Paid plans start at $19 per month and offer additional features such as no ads, private uploads, analytics, and buzz tracking to see who is sharing your content on sites like Twitter and Facebook.

179

It's Not the Tool;
It's the Content

Seth Godin is an innovator, author, marketer, and early adopter of blogging. You might be familiar with his books *Linchpin, Tribes, The Dip,* and *Purple Cow,* which contain new ways of thinking about marketing and leadership and challenge how we look at the world we live in today. Seth says, "Communication is the transfer of emotion."[4] Seth Godin has some pretty strong opinions about presentations, and he shares his five rules for presentations in one of his posts, "Really Bad PowerPoint."[5] One of his rules is to keep your slides free of excess words—six words is the maximum. He also dislikes spins and other fancy transitions and recommends against what he calls "cheesy images."

Success Stories

Every day there are new stories featuring creative, risk-taking, bold job seekers who have caught the attention of recruiters and hiring managers. Here are just a couple for you to think about.

Company-Specific Campaigns

Presentations created to attract the attention of a specific audience work well, if the audience sees it. Perhaps the following story, shared on the career page of the software company VMware about one of its new hires, will inspire you.[6]

Hanna Phan, an IT engineer, wanted to work at SlideRocket, which, by the way, is a maker of presentation software products. Hanna knew a standard resume wasn't going to set her apart in the competitive job market, so she created a SlideRocket presentation, of course. Hanna created her presentation resume and sent out the following tweet to the CEO of SlideRocket, Chuck Dietrich.

> "@chuckdietrich @sliderocket I want to work with you! Find my application here: http://portal.sliderocket.com/AIWCI/Iwanttoworkatsliderocket"[7]
>
> An hour later, after Chuck literally walked off a plane, he replied:
>
> "@hannaphan @sliderocket AMAZING Preso! Let's talk."[8]

Hanna had wowed SlideRocket with her out-of-the-box presume and landed the product manager job.

As you can see, it wasn't enough for Hanna to hope SlideRocket would see her presentation. She purposefully shared it with the CEO. Also note the name of her SlideRocket presentation—"Iwanttowork atsliderocket." Clearly, Hanna's interest helped set her apart as well as her talent.

If you are thinking you might like to test SlideRocket for your presentation, note that as of June 2013, SlideRocket has integrated with ClearSlide. In doing so, its presentation platform has become more narrowly focused to address sales leaders and teams in various ways pitching and marketing—and therefore less accessible and relevant for your job search.

Going Viral

Of course, there is always the chance your presentation could go viral. Such was the case for Jordan McDonnell, a financial analyst seeking a new, more creative role. Jordan created a presentation-style resume titled "This Is NOT my resume" and uploaded it to SlideShare. Unexpectedly, Jordan's CV went viral and to date has over 250,000 views, 90,000-plus views accumulated within nine days. Job offers came in from around the world, but it was a position as an account manager with Twitter in his hometown of Dublin, Ireland, that Jordan selected.[9] Jordan's original presentation has since been updated; you can see his current version here: http://www.slideshare.net/jmcdcems/this-is-not-my-resume.

181

Alice Lee, a University of Pennsylvania student, desperately wanted to work for Instagram, and so she skipped classes to make a website "Dear Instagram" to showcase her programming and design skills, as well as her love for photography and web start-ups. Alice's site caught the attention of media and went viral and resulted in a phone call from the CEO. Though she wasn't offered a position with Instagram, Alice did land an internship with Path, a company in a similar market to that of Instagram.[10]

Step Up Your Game

If you are tired of playing the same old game of applying for jobs online and waiting, maybe taking an approach like these job seekers did will make a difference. Stepping outside your comfort zone may be just the solution. If taking such a big step seems overwhelming or frightening, maybe dipping into the social media waters is a bit less intimidating, yet just as beneficial.

CHAPTER 11

Choose What You Share Online Carefully

The chances of getting a call from a recruiter merely because you've created a flashy marketing piece using one of the tools mentioned in previous chapters are slim. You need to call attention to what you've created. You have to distribute your message. Marketing and sales are a part of managing your career and proactively searching for a job.

In Chapter 9 you read that 93 percent of recruiters are likely to look at a candidate's social profile[1] to assess professional experience, length of professional tenure, specific hard skills, cultural fit, and industry-related posts.

Let's take a look at how you can get on the radar of hiring managers, recruiters, and HR professionals.

How would someone get on your radar?

Arie Ball, VP Talent Acquisition at Sodexo,[2] told Glassdoor that in order to get on her radar, it's important the individual has something to show. Ball says, "I tend to notice professionals who are actively engaged in their profession, and contribute in a thoughtful way to discussions. Who can help but notice professionals with a true passion for their work, or for causes they believe in?"

Do Recruiters Really Care What You Are Saying Online?

Recruiters do want to learn more about you to make sure you'll be a good fit for the role. That's why they conduct phone screening interviews. However, in many cases, recruiters are pressed for time, and investigating the social profiles of all applicants to assess their skills and fit just isn't feasible. Let's say a recruiter receives a resume and it is packed with all the right qualifications for the job. The next step the recruiter takes is to reach out to the candidate, usually by phone or sometimes by e-mail, to learn more. If a seemingly qualified candidate has included links to a portfolio or social networking profiles, the recruiter could, based on interest and preferences, easily click through to evaluate the candidate further. If there aren't any links, the recruiter would have to invest more time seeking out the candidate's online activity.

Recruiters have different preferences for when or if they'll scope out a candidate. They may run a quick Google search or social profile check before, during, or after their outreach to the candidate. Your goal is to make every recruiter's job easier by making your information readily accessible.

Historically, you would have to make it to the interview phase to show how you perform when on your best behavior, but now an employer can catch a candid glimpse of how you communicate and what's important to you before the interview, potentially saving time. Your viewable (public) posts, forum discussions, comments, and other activities, like sharing photos on Instagram or checking into places with FourSquare, help paint a picture of the real you—personally and professionally.

Some recruiters may start their search for candidates by using LinkedIn. Recruiters will search for profiles that contain the right level of experience and skills. Only after they have found qualified potential recruits will the recruiters be interested in learning more and want to dive deeper to investigate. Remember, recruiters have immediate access to the information people publicly share in their profile, through status updates, and in group discussions. If recruiters see a demonstration of skills through examples of work, active group discussion, glowing testimonials, and intelligent status updates, they've hit the jackpot.

So do recruiters care what you are saying? Yes and no. They do want to learn more about you, and sooner in the process is better than later. But first they have to see enough evidence or proof that you could do the job. In an ideal world, recruiters would have the time and inclination to thoroughly research every candidate that applied. But this isn't always the case. Some recruiters are as busy as one-armed paper hangers, doing everything possible to fill open job requisitions. These recruiters are not as likely to take time to click through on links or research you online.

These are generalities. No two recruiters follow exactly the same process or have the same steps for evaluating candidates. What you should know is that if you don't make it easy to see your work by including links within your resume and LinkedIn profile, you are leaving it to chance they will find the information.

Prominent Social Networks

The five popular social networks you should be aware of for your job search are LinkedIn, Twitter, Facebook, Google+, and Pinterest. You may be familiar with LinkedIn, the most popular social network for professionals. But there are advantages to using other networks as well. Twitter and Google+ are open networks, which means that you can see and respond to anyone's public status updates. The advantage to you is that you don't need to be connected to or be friends with someone to comment on the person's status update or news he or she is sharing. Facebook and LinkedIn are networks based on connections and relationships; therefore, if you want to communicate directly with someone on either of those networks, you need to be connected. If you don't have many connections or friends, this limits your ability to communicate with potential employers outside of your network.

Independent Adoption of Social Media

Pew Internet & American Life Project, an organization that provides information by conducting public opinion polling and social science research, reports that 72 percent of online adults use social networking sites, according to 2013 research.[3] This means that most of you reading this book already are using social networks, but you may not have thought to use them to help your career and job search.

You don't necessarily need to be active on all the social networks, but you will learn what you can do to stand out in case you do choose to use social media.

Company Adoption of Social Media

Increasingly, recruiters and employers are seeing the advantages of having active communities on social networks. According to the University of Massachusetts Dartmouth Center for Marketing Research, 34 percent of Fortune 500 companies are now actively blogging, 77 percent maintain active Twitter accounts, 70 percent have Facebook pages, and 69 percent have YouTube accounts.[4]

Plan What You'll Talk About Online

Just building a social network profile or infographic resume without giving thought to how you will use it is unlikely to attract the attention you hope for. In Chapter 12, you will find tips for tracking what's working and what's not.

Before you build your social resume or share links to your social networks, you should think about what your social network updates will look like. You are giving permission and access to recruiters and hiring entities to look at your stream, so ask yourself, what would they like to see? Consider categorizing the things you share into these four types of updates:

- Showcase your expertise (self-promotional).
- Prove you have responsible and emotionally intelligent communication skills.
- Show you are staying up-to-date on industry trends and news.
- Prove you have personality and style.

If you are pursuing a marketing role, you may want to show you can launch, manage, and track campaign results. You could share a link to a case study you prepared and uploaded on SlideShare showing how you managed a recent campaign or project. This may be a class project, a project accomplished during an internship, or even your job search campaign.

If you are pursuing a role with a customer service component, the recruiter will most likely look for evidence that you have good follow-up and customer communication skills. You could share a link to a recent customer testimonial (with permission, of course) or link to the recommendations on your LinkedIn profile as a status update to show off an award or new recommendation.

A single update about one current event won't necessarily capture the heart and mind of a recruiter. Instead it will be the overall impression that recruiters get from reading your stream or all your visible updates. Be aware and thoughtful and consider the four types of updates that will create balance in the information you share online.

Share Industry News

You can supply proof of your special areas of knowledge by sharing articles or recent industry news. Sharing relevant news shows you are up-to-date, and it provides evidence that you are a team player of sorts or at least help others. You can find these through LinkedIn news you've chosen to follow, SmartBrief articles, industry news from Technorati, or featured blogs on AllTop, or you can subscribe to industry newsletters or publications. All these provide great content ready to share. Another option is to participate in group discussions on LinkedIn by answering someone's question or providing a helpful resource, as, for example:

> "New financial update from @federalreserve. Will this impact globally? [insert link]"

Share Events or Activities You Participate In

You can write a status update referencing an event you are attending such as an industry conference, MeetUp, presentation, or networking event. Your updates could address key points or take-aways from the event or give a well-deserved compliment to the presenter by using the person's name or social network handle. An example might look like this:

> "Great job @LindaJ! Learned a ton today during #teacher's webinar on classroom survival tactics. Here's the preso [insert link]"

188

Showing your support for an organization you volunteer with speaks to your outside interests. You can share the organization's news or events with your network, which also helps create awareness of the organization's work. Here is a sample:

> "Just renewed membership with @AMA_Marketing Best money I've spent all year! Can't wait for San Diego conference in March."

Find and Follow Online Talent Communities

You've probably noticed recruiters saying, in this book and elsewhere, that they want you to engage with them online. Many companies mention their social media outlets on their website or blog. Some may even have special accounts for careers. Once you join these communities, watch what is being posted, post thoughtful questions to the discussion, and look for opportunities to share some industry news or congratulate the company on a recent accomplishment, award, or initiative.

Also take note of the employees interacting in the talent communities and follow their personal accounts on social networks. Reach out and ask if you can connect on LinkedIn as well. In the near future, you will likely see more companies creating talent communities in order to build a pool of potential candidates to draw from. Talent communities can be a lower cost alternative to sourcing new hires.

What to Avoid Saying Online

What types of things work against you on social profiles? The top six negative influence topics, according to a Jobvite study,[5] include references to doing illegal drugs, sexual updates, profanity, spelling and grammar errors, references to guns, and pictures of consumption of alcohol.

Be aware of how you behave online and avoid getting into arguments or criticizing people. Stay away from making negative comments of any kind anywhere, especially updates or comments referencing your current or past employers. These automatically reflect poorly on your professionalism.

189

Politics and religion are generally taboo topics. You don't know the beliefs of the people reviewing your content, and you certainly don't want to offend anyone. Though Jobvite's survey found recruiters were indifferent to seeing these posts and updates in candidates' streams, it would be wise to avoid sharing extreme views or opinions on these topics.

Location updates on sites like Foursquare might send an unfavorable message. For example, if you are "checking in" at your favorite bar every day, think about what impression that makes on a future employer. The music, videos, and images you share and like should also be rated G and appropriate for all audiences. You can argue that what you do during your free time is your business and shouldn't be used against you. The reality is, if you've put it out there publicly, it is fair game for judgment.

Attract Attention with Hashtags

A hashtag is a way to tag or flag a message. You may have seen hashtags used across Twitter, Facebook, Instagram, and Google+, primarily because they make the status update searchable. This means anyone who wants to see updates or profiles flagged by #visualcv can go to the search bar on Twitter, Facebook, Instagram, or Google+ and search for any profile or update tagged with that hashtag. As a job seeker, you can search for "#job" and see anyone's public status update that includes the hashtag #job. You may also want to search for "#infographic" and see who's using that hashtag.

Socially savvy recruiters use "#job" to flag posted opportunities. They also might use a hashtag before the job title for increased searchability, such as "#analyst," "#payroll," or "#HR." Think about using these hashtags:

- **#hireme.** This is a direct call to action for anyone wanting to promote his or her availability for work or anyone interested in helping spread your message.

- **#MBA.** A hashtag like this should attract employers looking for MBA-level candidates.
- **#profile.** This clearly flags that you're sharing your profile in your status update.
- **#resume.** If you're tweeting about your resume posted online, be sure to insert a hashtag like this.
- **#visualcv.** And if you are sharing your visual or infographic resume, this will call attention to it.

Proactive Targeting

> ### Was there a candidate that totally wow-ed you and if yes, how did they do it?
>
> "Yes, my current intern. She DM'd me on Twitter and got the job!" This is what Talent Warrior Jeremy Langhans, manager of Global Talent Acquisition at Expedia, told Glassdoor.[6]

Only 20 percent of jobs are filled through job boards.[7] So how will you find out about jobs if they aren't advertised this way? It starts by creating a list of companies you think you would like to work for.

Conducting a proactive search requires that you do more than just spray-and-pray your resume to hundreds of job postings. Strong sales professionals create prospect lists. These lists contain the company and contact information of people who *may* be interested in their product or service in the future. In your case, we'll call these prospects "target companies." Your list of target companies could potentially need your skills or expertise.

You probably do have some idea of places you would like to work or a job or two you would be interested in. Maybe it is a company you've heard about in the news or have heard people rave about. This is a starting point. You have to trust in the exploration process. This list of resources may help you discover great companies:

191

- Look at Glassdoor.com's Best Places to Work.
- Check out Fortune's 100 Best Companies to Work For.
- Search the Internet for "Top 100" and "Best Employer" lists for your city.

Let's say you would love to work for Google because it is innovative, it sounds like a good place to work, and most importantly, Google hires people who do what you do.

Now that you have at least one company you would like to work for, identify what industry it is in so you can find similar companies and take note of who its competitors are. Similar companies and competitors will likely have similar job opportunities. Hoovers (only basic-level information is free), Yahoo Finance, and LinkedIn are just three of many resources to help you identify similar companies and competitors.

There are lots of research tools out there, and your local library may be able to help you research companies within a specific industry—libraries have access to databases you may not, such as ReferenceUSA.

The hope is that you will have many companies on your list, and that's okay. Actually, it is better to have more than not enough. Focus on the top 10 first. For each of your top 10 targets, take the following steps:

- Follow the career or job posting page on the company's website.
- Follow the company page on LinkedIn.
- Like the company page and career page on Facebook.
- Follow the company Twitter accounts.
- Add the company to your Google+ circles.
- Reach out to employees you know in target companies across all social networks.
- Share news and articles mentioning your targets.
- Comment on blogs or articles written by your target companies.
- Ask and answer questions on group or community pages where employees belong.

Do the Two-Step

How many times have you simply applied for a job and left your application in the hands of fate? Is there anything you can do to increase the odds that someone will actually review your resume?

Step One

Most job applicants won't take the time to do these two steps, and that's the very reason you should. The first step is easy. You find a job online and research the company and the opportunity so you completely understand what the company is looking for. Then you modify your resume to showcase the most important qualifications you have for the job and attach a cover letter that explains why you want to work at that company.

Step Two

Step two requires you to find someone who works for that company. Though it sounds like a simple idea, it can be time consuming to implement.

Your mission is to find a strong ally, supporter, cheerleader, or advocate inside the company. This will increase the odds of your resume getting reviewed. It is called an employee referral, and it is powerful. According to the 2013 CareerXroads source-of-hiring study, the number one source of external hiring was employee referrals at 24.5 percent![8] This is why step two is so important. You are leveraging the power of an inside contact to refer you.

Step two provides a great opportunity for you to forward your infographic resume or social resume to someone inside the company, even if you have already submitted your formal application. What you are attempting to do now is gain support. The employees you reach out to may appreciate the creative documentation or novel approach. Just be sure to let your inside connections know you've submitted a formal resume through their company's application process and you would be happy to share it with them too.

The referral process may work differently depending on the company. In order for an employee referral to work properly, the employee

193

may need to submit your resume or you may need to use the employee's name when you complete the application. The best course of action is to check with the person inside the company before you formally apply.

Use the Power of LinkedIn

LinkedIn is the go-to source for finding what are known as inside connections—people who work at your target companies. When you go to a company's page on LinkedIn, see who works there and whom you are connected to. If your network is tiny, that is, if you have fewer than 100 connections on LinkedIn, finding first-level connections is going to be tough.

On a side note, your LinkedIn connections should mirror your real-life connections. If you think about it, you have probably interacted with more than 100 other professionals over the past couple of years. You should have at least this many connections in your network. But this isn't just a number game. The strength of your relationships is equally important.

Don't Stop There

Twitter, Facebook, Google+, and Pinterest all draw different crowds and may enable you to tap into employees who work for the company you are applying to. Search them all.

Unlike LinkedIn, Twitter and Google+ are open networks that don't require someone to accept your invitation to connect. You can freely follow people's accounts and see what they are saying on these platforms. The benefit to you is that you can or could begin immediately building a relationship with company insiders without waiting for a referral, as you usually would on LinkedIn. Google+ has its own built-in search functionality using the search bar. You can use the following tools to help search Twitter profiles:

TWITTER SEARCH TOOLS

- FollowerWonk (http://followerwonk.com/bio)
- Twellow (http://www.twellow.com)
- JustTweetIt (http://justtweetit.com)

How to Share Your Infographic Resume

The famous line from *Field of Dreams*, "Build it and they will come," isn't necessarily true for resumes. In order for people to find your infographic resume, or anything else you create to market your talent, you need to attract their attention. By following these recommendations, you can create a buzz around your infographic resume and perhaps generate the same results as some of the success stories mentioned in this book.

Name It Wisely

The Internet is one big database of information. When people want to find answers or are looking for something (or someone), they enter words or phrases into the search bar. When naming your infographic resume, or anything else you plan to upload online, you will most likely want it to include your name and perhaps your occupation too. Taking this approach will help ensure that someone searching for your name will find most, if not all, of your online documentation.

In the example in Chapter 10, Hanna Phan named her presentation "Iwanttoworkatsliderocket." This approach worked because she had created a presentation especially designed with that particular company in mind, and one of the activities socially savvy companies do is monitor the Internet for all references to their own name. Hanna's presentation would likely have shown up in their monitoring and perhaps been forwarded along internally. But in this case it didn't need that passive approach because Hanna tweeted it directly to the company's founder, who was instantly interested.

Give Your Infographic Resume a Home

If you have a website, the best location to post your infographic resume is on its own page on your site. This enables you to easily share and track the web address or URL. If you have created your infographic resume using one of the tools listed in Chapter 7, either your infographic can be downloaded, or your infographic's URL can

195

be hosted on the site. If you choose to let the site host it, then plan to share the link and embed it in your LinkedIn profile.

Get a Tumblr Page for Your Career

Tumblr is a microblogging site. The majority of people use it to share photos, images, and videos. If you do not have a website, this may be an option. You can upload your infographic resume, links to the text version of your resume, screenshots of your social resumes, and the many other visuals you collect for your online portfolio, and you can share them all here. Once your images have been uploaded to your post on Tumblr, you can share the link back to this page on Facebook, Pinterest, or other social networks. It is just one more place for you to establish a foothold on the Internet.

Share It with Your Network

When you share your infographic resume or any career marketing tools with the people in your network, be sure you ask for their support. In order for the folks in your network to do exactly what you want them to, you should provide clear directions. If you just want them to like your work, tell them. However, if you would like them to share it with people they know or as their own status update, you will have to make that request. For example:

> "Pls share, like, and distribute freely to your network! Jane Doe #InfograhicResume [link]"

Share It with People at Target Companies

When you find the Google+ or Twitter account for people who work for one of your target companies, reach out by just saying hello. Next, read their profile and see what types of content they've shared or what topics they are talking about. Look for opportunities to reshare their updates, or share relevant interests with them. Throwing your infographic resume at them as your first form of interaction could potentially be a turn-off. After you've had an exchange, even a thank you from them, you might share a public tweet that says:

196

"Sam @SamatXYZco thanks for following—hey have you seen what I've been up to? [link]"

or

"Would love to chat about your UI experience @SamatXYZco. The newest frames are great!"

Post It Everywhere and Often

As you can see from Philippe Dubost's success in Chapter 4, his infographic created quite a buzz. It generated over 39,000 likes on Facebook. The best strategy is to post your infographic resume on as many social networks as possible. Pinterest, Instagram, Tumblr, and Flickr are all great networks for sharing visual content, especially infographics. StumbleUpon and Reddit are sites where users recommend and share content (articles, images, and other media) with other users. Based on your interests, you can easily sort and filter the popular topics and articles being shared. In order to share your infographic on any of these sites, you will need a free account. Once you've set that up, sharing your infographic resume is as easy as using the share button on the infographic tool you used to create it or copying and pasting the URL of your infographic into the site's submit box.

Create a Pinboard for Your Career Documentation

Pinterest received notoriety for being the fastest-growing social network ever, as reported by TechCrunch.[9] And Pinterest currently places as the third largest social network in terms of users, according to "The 2012 Digital Marketer: Benchmark and Trend Report" released by Experien, a marketing services company.[10] In case you aren't familiar with this tool, Pinterest users create online scrapbooks made from photos they find online or upload. Users can browse other pinboards for images, "repin" images to their own pinboards, or like photos. This makes Pinterest an ideal place for you to upload your infographic resume. Why not create an entire pinboard dedicated to showcasing your career achievements and label it with your

197

name and occupation, as, for example, "Jane Doe—Administrative Support and Customer Advocate." Include your intelligently labeled infographic and mark it as the board's cover for extra viewing power.

Instagram Updates

Instagram is primarily a tool for sharing pictures and videos. While most people use it from a mobile device (iPhone or Android phone), you can also upload files from your PC to your Instagram feed. Chop your infographic resume into parts and share, because your whole image would be too small to decipher. Once you post something to your feed, it is publicly viewable to anyone on Instagram, and this is exactly what you want. To help attract attention to your uploaded infographic, use an appropriate hashtag like "#infographicresume," "#infographiccv," or just "#infographic."

SlideShare Hosts Infographics Too

SlideShare hosts presentations, documents, and even infographics, so be sure to upload your infographic resume here as well. If you haven't done so already, uploading a pdf of your text resume to SlideShare is a good idea. First, when people search for information on the Internet or on SlideShare, your document is publicly searchable— and that means findable. Second, if you've ever been away from your computer and wished you could send your resume to someone, you'll appreciate the fact that you can easily share the URL to your resume on SlideShare.

Leverage Infographic Sharing Sites

The sites listed below are specifically designed to feature infographics and serve as directories for people looking for infographics or those who want to promote an infographic. If you want to increase the number of people who could potentially see and share your infographic, it makes sense to post it to as many places as possible.

Michael David, founder of TasteyPlacement, an Internet marketing and infographic development company, recommends sharing your infographic within directories focused on infographics such as those listed below:[11]

- Infographics Archive (http://www.infographicsarchive.com/submit-infographics/)
- Submit Infographics (http://submitinfographics.com/)
- Infographic Site (http://infographicsite.com/submit-infographic/)
- Visual.ly (http://visual.ly)
- Reddit Infograhics (http://reddit.com/r/infographics/)
- Nerd Graph (http://www.nerdgraph.com/submit-infographic/)
- Infographic Love (http://www.infographiclove.com)

These are some more directories you may want to explore and test out:

- Daily Infographic (http://dailyinfographic.com/)
- Cool Infographics (http://www.coolinfographics.com/)
- Visual Loop (http://visualoop.tumblr.com/)

Pulling It All Together

The logic explained in the preceding pages will ensure that the social network links referenced on your social resume are "publishable" or "shareable."

Promoting your infographic or any other online content requires expending some amount of effort and knowing where to go to share. Marketing yourself to the appropriate target audience and increasing the awareness of your skills and talents rests in your hands. Your next step is to monitor the results of your hard work.

199

CHAPTER 12

Numbers Speak

It only takes one interested employer to offer you the right job. That's the only number that really counts in the long run, but this isn't the only number that matters. The number of views received by your profile, infographic resume, or other content matters a lot. If a recruiter is searching anywhere online for someone with your skill set, you want that recruiter to find you. When you have a visible online presence, it will increase the odds of the recruiter finding you. You want to ensure that the right employer sees your stunning infographic or profile. In this chapter, you'll see what questions to ask yourself and what to evaluate to see if your personal marketing campaign is working.

Your First Priority

Your top priority is to create targeted, eye-catching, relevant content. This was the focus of the book, and now you are ready to create your work using the inspiration from examples I've shared with you on previous pages.

One of the best strategies for creating compelling marketing materials is to customize your content for your audience. When you look at the successful stories about job seekers who caught the attention of their dream employer, it was because they crafted a unique message to that very specific company. The pitch, resume, or outreach targeted the employer and spelled out exactly why the individual wanted to work for that employer. The message presented by each candidate clearly defined what the candidate could do to help that employer and provided supporting evidence to prove the match with the company, its job, and the culture.

Your Second Priority

Share your work. This is your chance. Everyone wants the proverbial 15 seconds of fame. Give legs to your social resume, infographic resume, portfolio, or LinkedIn profile by sharing it on popular social networks and news-sharing sites. This doesn't guarantee a major media outlet will pick up your material, but it does increase the reach and potential exposure.

Your Third Priority—Monitor How Many Views You Get

When someone views your link, it generally means there is some level of interest. Almost all of the portfolio, profiles, and networks include some form of analytics. Most will list how many views your profile or update receives. Assessing the number of views helps you evaluate if you used the right keywords, which means your content was discovered through a search. If your status updates included a message that enticed the reader to click on the link, this would also be a measure of success and something to replicate.

Sites like LinkedIn, Pinterest, Facebook, and About.me allow users to like an image that has been shared or a status update. The number of likes is a form of endorsement. Monitor how many people like your work over a period of time, maybe two weeks. If you don't see the number of views increase, especially after you've shared your visual resume as an update, then you'll need to determine if it was your post content or the image itself.

Infographic directories, such as Visual.ly, track and show number of views, faves, and the overall rank of an infographic. You will see similar analytics on most of the design communities, such as Behance, which allows community members to give a project a thumbs-up and add specific feedback in comments.

If you have posted your infographic on a site with social sharing icons, you can see the number of shares to the social networks supported, such as Facebook, Digg, or numerous other popular sites.

An increase in the number of people who have viewed your content should generate more phone calls or e-mails to you. This is the next level to assess. How many people are reaching out to you or trying to connect or contact with you. You want the number of views and the quantity of outreach to you to both increase. If this isn't happening, you'll want to investigate why. Have you oversold or undersold your qualifications? What are they seeing when they view your online content that makes them *not* want to pick up the phone and call you? As you can see, generating interest is a multiple-step process.

No Tracking, No Problem

When analytics are not available, there is another way for you to track how many people share, click, and view your page. URL shorteners like bit.ly or Google allow you to assign a unique URL to a page. Just copy the URL or web address for the page you want to share, and paste it into the shortener tool. When you share your shortened links, the code-shortening provider supplies analytics, reporting the number of clicks, views, and shares for that specific link. Now, when you share the shortened link to your infographic resume, you can easily see analytics across all the places you've shared it—from one dashboard.

Social Proof Through Measurement

PeerIndex and Klout measure your social influence. Each has its own formula for calculating the influence you have by evaluating the number of shares, reshares, and conversations you have online. An additional element used in the formulas is the influence level of people you interact with and who share your information. The more influential people apparently positively impact your social influence as well.

Some companies have been known to research candidates' PeerIndex and Klout scores to evaluate the activity on social networks. Generally, the companies doing this are evaluating candidates for jobs requiring a level of mastery of social media tools and resources.

PeerIndex and Klout accounts are free to create and help you evaluate your social activity in comparison with others. To set up an account, you will need to link to your various social networks, which will be used to calculate your score.

You may want to consider checking these sites on a regularly scheduled basis, very much the way you would your credit score. This is a form of monitoring your social credit. Knowing where you stand is better than a surprise down the road or one raised by an employer during the interview.

Take Corrective Action Before It's Too Late

When you monitor the results of your efforts, you can make adjustments in case what you are doing doesn't work. For example, if you send a Tweet with your LinkedIn profile and it doesn't get shared or clicked on, evaluate these factors:

- Have you used the right keywords?
- Did you post your status update too early or too late in the day or on an off day?
- Did you use a hashtag?
- Did you ask for a retweet, share, or comment?
- Do you post too often or not often enough?

There is some experimentation that has to take place. And what may have worked well one time may not work the next. Mix up when and how you share updates and monitor your results.

Tap into Objective Resources

Analytically reviewing your results and tweaking your activities might require advice from an objective outsider. Pull together a team of friends you can count on to offer that objective perspective.

Your Campaign
Never Truly Ends

You've got the steps down—create visual content, share it, and monitor how many people are viewing it. Are the numbers growing? The good news is that you know all the work you've put forth will make a difference in how many people see your work and learn about you. The bad news: your campaigning never ends. You will need a new job again. It will take less time to get noticed next time because you've been keeping your campaign running, perhaps not at the same pace, but your new career requires constant self-promotion on the job and outside your company.

Conclusion

What I hope you have found throughout this book is that the power to communicate in new and broader forms is now in your hands. Your resume and information about your work experience no longer need to reside in a folder, on your desktop, or in the black hole of applicant tracking systems. It is possible that you could land your next job because a recruiter stumbles across your infographic resume while browsing Pinterest. Or an employer wanting to hire someone with work experience like yours found your social resume while doing a Google search. Or perhaps a friend of a friend was so enamored with your infographic resume that he or she forwarded it along to numerous contacts and friends.

The resources to disperse and promote your career achievements are expanding. Most of the tools in this book are free and rely on your creativity, not your financial resources.

Some thought leaders in the career space have said the paper resume is dead or dying. What we know is that the hiring landscape is changing, and even the definition of career is morphing. I would like to conclude with these key points, which serve as important take-aways and actions from this book.

The Quest for Talent

It is predicted that employers will continue to have difficulty finding exactly the right talent to fill their vacancies. In the recruiting industry, this elusive candidate with a difficult-to-find skill set is often referred to as a purple squirrel. Imagine thousands of squirrels running around searching for nuts. Those are the unemployed or underemployed workers. But the employer is looking for a purple one. Is there even such a variety? Unlikely. So in order to improve the odds of a candidate landing a job, there needs to be a clear match between the skills delivered and the realistically assessed skills needed. The traditional application process is jammed with resumes, of which 50 percent are deemed unqualified according to recruiters.[1] The problem is twofold. Job seekers may not be communicating their skills in terms or specifics valued by employers, and most job descriptions are void of the details necessary for job seekers to identify what is really required of a job. Visual, infographic, and social resumes offer hope in bridging this communication gap.

Reach Out and Stand Out

Sitting back and submitting your resume through online applicant tracking systems is almost an exercise in futility. Remember some of the success stories in this book and what the job seekers did to set themselves apart. Some took initiative to reach out to company leaders through social networks; others created a viral buzz that caught the attention of multiple employers. If you want to compete for jobs today, you will have to do more than the minimum. Every resume, portfolio, and resource in this book is dedicated to doing more than what is expected. It is what you do with this information and how you distribute or market your materials that determine how successful your materials are in reaching the right target employers.

Create and Innovate

My hope is that the examples in this book help you to think outside of the old-fashioned job search box and beyond the traditional resume. Begin today creating or capturing visual proof of your career accomplishments. Perhaps you will find new ways to use an infographic resume or develop a new type of chart to show off your experience. Mobile technology and visual storytelling are today's fads. Yes, there will be new trends, but it is difficult to predict what they will be. The new career mode is to keep moving forward and embrace change, personally and professionally.

Proactively Manage Your Career

Pay attention to the demand for new skills in your occupation and industry and take initiative to stay up-to-date. Job seekers who have had success landing jobs faster tend to share some common traits. They are relationship builders, take calculated risks, and have taken their career destiny into their own hands. It is predicted that you will have dozens of different jobs over your lifetime, so looking for a new

209

job is an activity you will get accustomed to. Your job search is not a "once-and-done" activity. In order to be prepared for the next one, continue gathering testimonials of your work, clip web articles referencing your achievements, and be sure as many people as possible inside your organization are aware of what you've accomplished.

Hiring Is Ultimately About Likability

Networking is the top way people get jobs, as much as you may not want to hear it. Networking, at its very core, is about building relationships, and relationships are based on shared interests, trust, and likability. Social networking tools make it easier for people to connect and develop relationships. Developing new relationships is why so many companies have begun using social media to engage with potential employees. It is fast, free, and relatively painless. Come up the curve and learn about new social networks—your relationships will grow and benefit.

Look Outside Your Industry for Trends and Ideas

All industries have unique characteristics. Sometimes if you've been embedded in one industry, it is easy to become complacent and miss some of the ideas being adopted in other industries. So, if you get stuck in a rut in your job or even your search for a new job, take a step back and see what your job looks like in a different company and within a different industry. You may just gain some new ideas.

Maximize Tools to Simplify the Work

This book references numerous tools you can use to develop, create, curate, or aggregate your career documentation and provide proof you can deliver results. If you don't have the design skills to create an infographic resume, don't invest your valuable time learning if it doesn't serve you well. Instead, leverage the infographic tools that create an infographic from your LinkedIn information to simplify the project. If you aren't happy with those results, enlist the help of a professional. Each minute or day that you let pass by without your new documentation in place is limiting your access to opportunities.

Rather than feel overwhelmed by all the social networks, focus on LinkedIn first and master that language before embarking on new foreign territories. There's a theory saying that if you master one foreign language first, it becomes easier to learn others. Test this theory with the languages of social networks too.

Diversify Your Marketing Materials

Now is the time to future-proof your career. Begin investing in new marketing materials that will attract new audiences. Not everyone wants to see or knows how to use an infographic resume, but for visual learners (about half the population), your new visual resume could be just the tool they need to see to understand what skills and experience you offer.

Images Are Powerful

An indisputable trend is the growing importance of visual content. Images transcend words, make information simple to comprehend, and pack a powerful, memorable punch. Remember, six seconds is all the time an average recruiter gives to scan your resume.[2]

Your Real-Time Resume Is on the Web

You are being Googled. Employers are researching you online, and that information is much more easily accessible than your resume. News mentioning you, comments you've left on popular websites, Amazon book reviews, social network updates and profiles, articles you've written, and presentations you've delivered—all these mentions become your real-time resume. And what you need to know is that you can influence what content is viewable and what content you want people to find. It all starts with an awareness and benchmark of what can be found today. Each day you have new opportunities to develop an online reputation of excellence by creating web content for a blog or industry newsletter or by adding professional photos or images to your social network updates or Flickr. It is about being purposeful in the stream of content you share and create to build the on-brand, best-of-the-best reputation.

Build the Right Digital Dirt

Creating the right digital dirt means you've given thought to how you can showcase your skills, experience, and accomplishments. It means you regularly monitor what shows up online about you and collect and curate screenshots and testimonials to showcase who you are and what you've accomplished.

Final Checklist

If you've gotten this far in the book, you deserve a reward for your effort! I've pulled all the pieces together here and outlined a checklist of action items to guide you through the process.

☐ Google yourself and see what comes up on the first few pages of search results.

☐ Maximize your LinkedIn profile and incorporate visual proof of your expertise. (Chapter 8)

☐ Create About.me, Vizualize.me, Re.vu, and Flavors.me pages and link them to your website, LinkedIn profile, Google+ profile, and e-mail signatures. (Chapter 9)

☐ Regularly create a status update across all your social network profiles and share a blend of news about you, your industry, and events.

☐ Create a master copy of your text-based resume to use just in case. (Chapter 4)

☐ Transform your traditional resume into an infographic resume to distribute directly to hiring managers. (Chapters 4–6)

☐ Circulate your visual or infographic resume to as many people as you can, and link it to your LinkedIn profile, website, and other social networks.

☐ Monitor the activity of your online content and look for opportunities to connect with people who have viewed your information. (Chapter 12)

Stay Connected and Informed

During the process of writing this book, resumes have moved, applications for infographic resumes have disappeared, and new tools have been introduced. In order to make it easy for you to view the images in this book and to help keep you up-to-date, I've listed URLs for the images on my website. I will update and monitor these links to keep them current. You will also find lists and examples of new infographic resume tools on this page. If you like what you see, please share and comment.

I encourage you to stay in touch and share your own finished product with me through social media. You can find me here:

- **Career Sherpa blog** (http://www.careersherpa.net)
- **The Infographic Resume** (http://careersherpa.net/the-infographic-resume)
- **Twitter @careersherpa** (https://twitter.com/careersherpa)
- **LinkedIn** (https://www.linkedin.com/in/hannahmorgan)
- **Facebook** (https://www.facebook.com/careersherpa)
- **Google+** (https://plus.google.com/+HannahMorgan)
- **Pinterest** (http://www.pinterest.com/careersherpa)

NOTES

CHAPTER 1

1. http://www.careerxroads.com/news/SourcesOfHire2013.pdf, p. 22.
2. http://info.theladders.com/our-team/not-hearing-back-from
   -recruiters-we-know-why.
3. http://www.careerxroads.com/news/SourcesOfHire2013.pdf, p. 7.
4. http://www.nytimes.com/2013/01/28/business/employers-increasingly
   -rely-on-internal-referrals-in-hiring.html?_r=0.
5. http://www.careeradvisoryboard.org/public/uploads/2012/10/Job
   -Preparedness-Indicator-Executive-Summary_FINAL-10.16.12.pdf,
   p. 3.
6. http://www.careeradvisoryboard.org/public/uploads/2011/11/Job
   -Preparedness-Indicator-Executive-Summary.pdf.
7. http://www.careerbuilder.com/share/aboutus/pressreleasesdetail.aspx
   ?sd=12%2F27%2F2012&id=pr731&ed=12%2F31%2F2013.
8. http://blogs.hbr.org/2013/02/independent-work-may-be-inevit/.
9. http://pewinternet.org/Commentary/2012/February/Pew-Internet
   -Mobile.aspx.
10. http://en.wikipedia.org/wiki/Sheryl_Sandberg.
11. http://barnard.edu/headlines/transcript-and-video-speech-sheryl
    -sandberg-chief-operating-officer-facebook.
12. http://www.linkedin.com/about-us.
13. http://www.linkedin.com/about-us.

CHAPTER 2

1. http://www.glassdoor.com/blog/top-10-recruiters-share-impress.

CHAPTER 3

1. Daniel H. Pink, *To Sell Is Human: The Surprising Truth About Moving
   Others*, Riverhead Books, 2012, p. 158.
2. Pink, *To Sell Is Human*, pp. 170–171.
3. Pink, *To Sell Is Human*, pp. 171–172.
4. http://michaelhyatt.com/9-suggestions-for-taking-better-headshots
   .html.

5. Reid Hoffman and Ben Casnocha, *The Start-Up of You*, Crown Business, 2012, p. 29.

CHAPTER 4

1. http://www.careerbuilder.com/share/aboutus/pressreleasesdetail.aspx ?sd=7%2F11%2F2012&id=pr707&ed=12%2F31%2F2012.
2. http://info.theladders.com/our-team/you-only-get-6-seconds-of-fame -make-it-count.
3. http://www.careerbuilder.com/share/aboutus/pressreleasesdetail.aspx ?sd=7%2F11%2F2012&id=pr707&ed=12%2F31%2F2012 [http://www .careerbuilder.com/share/aboutus/pressreleasesdetail.aspx?sd=7%2F11 %2F2012&id=pr707&ed=12%2F31%2F2012].
4. http://www.thinktwiceinc.com/olio/articles/persuasion_article.pdf, p. 12.
5. http://phildub.tumblr.com/.
6. http://www.careerbuilder.com/share/aboutus/pressreleasesdetail.aspx ?sd=7%2F11%2F2012&id=pr707&ed=12%2F31%2F2012.

CHAPTER 5

1. http://www.academia.edu/1666724/The_Word-Hoard_of_English _and_the_Historical_Thesaurus by Marc Alexander.
2. http://www.insurance.lloydstsb.com/personal/general/mediacentre/ homehazards_pr.as.
3. http://blog.hubspot.com/insiders/infographic-marketing.
4. http://www.sourcecon.com/news/2013/04/09/who-will-win-the-war -for-resume-2-0-ten-visual-resume-tools-reviewed/.
5. http://en.wikipedia.org/wiki/Visual_thinking.
6. http://www.google.com/trends/explore?q=infographic#q=infographic &cmpt=q.

CHAPTER 7

1. http://graphicdesign.about.com/od/elementsofgooddesign/tp/ elements.htm.
2. http://www.entrepreneur.com/article/175428#ixzz2XF9rFBMk.
3. http://opinionator.blogs.nytimes.com/2012/08/08/hear-all-ye-people -hearken-o-earth/?utm_source=slashdot&utm_medium=slashdot &utm_campaign=slashdot&_r=0.

CHAPTER 8

1. http://recruiting.jobvite.com/resources/social-recruiting-reports-and
   -trends/, http://reach.bullhornreach.com/reach/cmsites/default/files/
   BullhornReach_2012ActivityReport.pdf.
2. http://www.careerxroads.com/news/SourcesOfHire2013.pdf.
3. "Jobvite Social Recruiting Survey Results 2013," p. 7.
4. http://blog.linkedin.com/2013/05/30/enrich-your-updates-on
   -linkedin-with-rich-media/
5. http://help.linkedin.com/app/answers/detail/a_id/34327.
6. http://cdn.theladders.net/static/images/basicSite/pdfs/TheLadders
   -EyeTracking-StudyC2.pdf.

CHAPTER 9

1. http://web.jobvite.com/Q313_SocialRecruitingSurvey_LandingPage
   .html.
2. http://www.glassdoor.com/blog/top-10-recruiters-share-impress/.
3. http://www.nngroup.com/articles/how-little-do-users-read/.
4. http://www.glassdoor.com/blog/top-10-recruiters-share-impress/.
5. http://blog.about.me/2013/09/06/next/.

CHAPTER 10

1. *Slide:ology: The Art and Science of Creating Great Presentations* by
   Nancy Duarte, pp. 2–9 (eBook excerpt).
2. http://blog.hubspot.com/blog/tabid/6307/bid/20496/5-Rules-for
   -Creating-Great-Presentations-from-NancyDuarte.aspx.
3. http://blog.hubspot.com/blog/tabid/6307/bid/34274/7-lessons-from
   -the-world-s-most-captivating-presenters-slideshare.aspx].
4. http://sethgodin.typepad.com/seths_blog/2007/01/really_bad_powe
   .html.
5. http://sethgodin.typepad.com/seths_blog/2007/01/really_bad_powe
   .html.
6. http://blogs.vmware.com/careers/2011/10/how-a-sliderocket-employee
   -landed-her-dream-job.html.
7. https://twitter.com/hannaphan/status/98091065856372736.
8. https://twitter.com/chuckdietrich/status/98180893633548289.
9. http://blog.hreonline.com/2013/03/04/rethinking-the-resume/.
10. http://www.parade.com/59873/heatherhuhman/5-creative-resumes
    -that-got-millennials-hired/.

CHAPTER 11

1. http://web.jobvite.com/Q313_SocialRecruitingSurvey_LandingPage
.html.

2. http://www.glassdoor.com/blog/top-10-recruiters-share-impress/.

3. http://pewinternet.org/Reports/2013/social-networking-sites.aspx.

4. http://www.umassd.edu/cmr/socialmediaresearch/2013fortune500/.

5. http://web.jobvite.com/Q313_SocialRecruitingSurvey_LandingPage
.html.

6. http://www.glassdoor.com/blog/top-10-recruiters-share-impress/.

7. http://www.careerxroads.com/news/SourcesOfHire2013.pdf, p. 7.

8. http://www.careerxroads.com/news/SourcesOfHire2013.pdf, p. 7.

9. http://techcrunch.com/2012/02/07/pinterest-monthly-uniques/.

10. http://go.experian.com/forms/experian-digital-marketer-2012?WT
.srch=PR_EMS_DigitalMarketer2012_040412_Download?send=yes.

11. http://www.tastyplacement.com/how-to-promote-an-infographic.

CONCLUSION

1. http://online.wsj.com/news/articles/SB1000142405297020462420457 1
78941034941330.

2. http://cdn.theladders.net/static/images/basicSite/pdfs/TheLadders
-EyeTracking-StudyC2.pdf.

FIGURE CREDITS

The following people have graciously granted me permission to include their illustrations in this book:

Kevin Luu, Figure 2-1, 26
Robin Flanigan, Figure 2-2, 27
Marci Diehl, Figure 3-1, 44
Randy Krum, Figure 3-2, 44
Paul Biedermann, Figure 3-3, 45
Kelly Weihs, Figure 4-2, 57
Kristen Roberts, Figure 4-3, 59
Adrienne Robenstine, Figure 4-4, 61
Kyle Bahr, Figure 4-5, 63
Steve Retka, Figure 4-6, 65
Phillippe Dubost, Figure 4-8, 68
Entropii/Zabisco, Figure 5-1, 74
Kevin Burton, Figure 5-2, 77, and Figure 8-2, 155
Sneha Kochak, Figure 5-3, 79
Colleen Havens, Figure 5-4, 83
Daniel Tewfik, Figure 5-5, 85
Anjana Jayaweera, Figure 5-6, 87
Sheng Fen Chien, Figure 5-7, 89
Brad Crabtree, Figure 5-8, 91
John A. Miller, Figure 5-9, 93
Mike-Anthony Saade, Figure 5-10, 95
Shirley Schutt, Figure 5-11, 97
Hagan Blount, Figure 5-12, 99
Paolo Zupin, Figure 5-13, 101

Greg Gonzalez, Figure 5-14, 103
Steve Williams, Figure 5-14a and 5-15b, 105
Michelle Campbell, Figure 5-16, 107
Eliza Doton, Figure 5-17, 109
Jason Toff, Figure 6-1, 113
Daniel Brienza, Figure 6-2, 115, and Figure 7-5, 132
Jean Denniston, Figure 6-3, 116
Lindsey Julian, Figure 6-4, 119
Richard Jefferson, Figure 6-5, 120
Massimiliano Crescioli, Figure 7-8, 137
Jennifer Mathews, Figure 7-9, 138
Samantha Landry, Figure 7-10, 139
Christopher Cribb, Figure 7-11, 141
Mike Lally, Figure 8-1, 155
Ian Ripley, Figure 9-1, 164
Maui Aguilar, Figure 9-2, 165
Rachel Miller, Figure 9-3, 165
Erik Reinertsen, Figure 9-4, 166
Natalie Tarpinian, Figure 9-5, 167
Robert Silvia, Figure 9-6, 167
Rik Panganiban, Figure 9-7, 168
Jackie Correa, Figure 9-8, 168
Chris Russell, Figure 9-9, 169

INDEX

225

ABOUT THE AUTHOR

HANNAH MORGAN
**Job Search and
Social Media
Strategist**
Career Sherpa.net

Hannah is a speaker and author who provides no-nonsense career advice; she serves as a guide through today's treacherous job search terrain. Hannah is passionate about keeping up with the latest trends in reputation management, social networking strategies, and other methods for standing out in today's competitive world.

Hannah is a nationally recognized influencer of proactive job search; her work has been featured in the *Huffington Post, USA Today, LifeHacker, Business Insider, U.S. News & World Report, BlogHer,* and numerous other media outlets. You can learn more about Hannah on Career Sherpa.net.

Hannah recently coauthored *Social Networking for Business Success: How to Turn Your Ideas into Income,* a book to help entrepreneurs and small-business owners market their products and services through social media.